New Coins From Old Gold, Or, Homely Hints From Holy Writ

NEW COINS FROM OLD GOLD.

NEW COINS FROM OLD GOLD;

OR,

HOMELY HINTS FROM HOLY WRIT.

BY

THOMAS CHAMPNESS.

LONDON:

HODDER AND STOUGHTON,

27, PATERNOSTER ROW.

MDCCCLXXVIII.

Hazell, Watson, and Viney, Printers, London and Aylesbury.

To

MY HONOURED FATHER,

CHARLES CHAMPNESS,

OF MANCHESTER,

THIS "OFFERING OF THE FIRST FRUITS"

IS

AFFECTIONATELY DEDICATED,

IN THE HOPE

THAT HE WILL SEE IN IT

SOME SLIGHT REWARD FOR TEACHING HIS CHILDREN

THAT

THE "GOLD OF THAT LAND IS GOOD."

47, CITY ROAD, LONDON,
1878.

PREFACE.

A GREAT preacher once said, "There is nothing new under the sun." We are not sure that we know what he meant, and it is a question whether we shall ever have the opportunity of asking him. Perhaps he meant that, in the world of ideas, as in matter, there is only a certain amount of capital, and that change the form as you will, you cannot add to the whole without you can create,—and few of us lay claim to that power.

It is in accordance with this idea that the title of the book was chosen. The writer does not claim to have found out how to make gold, but he thinks the coin bears his image and superscription. Nor does he claim literary merit, but feels anxious to do good, and especially to put some heart into Christian workers; and he will be glad if only he has learned "to speak a word in season to him that is weary."

CONTENTS.

		PAGE
I.	HOW AND WHERE TO BEGIN	1
II.	THE GRANARY OF GOD	12
III.	THE FARMER'S GIFT	21
IV.	THE HOLY TENT	32
V.	THE HOLY CHEST	44
VI.	THE TEMPTATION OF CHRIST	55
VII.	WINNING GOD'S BATTLES	66
VIII.	THE HEAVENLY WORKMAN	79
IX.	THE LADDER	91
X.	FINDING THE TRIBUTE MONEY	102
XI.	WAITING IN MERCY'S HOUSE	113
XII.	A GOOD MAN'S BAD SON	128
XIII.	GLEANING	142

CONTENTS.

		PAGE
XIV.	"VIRTUE IS GONE OUT OF ME" .	154
XV.	STONING THE GODS . . .	168
XVI.	THE HISTORY OF A LETTER .	179
XVII.	WORKING FOR THE KING . .	193
XVIII.	ROPES AND RAGS . . .	206
XIX.	THE LOST AXE	222
XX.	WORN ON THE HEART OF CHRIST .	
XXI.	THE BATTLE OF MICHMASH .	255

I.

HOW AND WHERE TO BEGIN.

JOHN ii. 1-11.

WHERE did Jesus begin? He must begin somewhere. Where is it to be? He had all the world before Him. Shall it be at Jerusalem? There will be a crowd of admirers. Yes, there will be a crowd, but that is just the difference between the Christ and impostors. He does not seek a large audience. There is no vulgarity about the chosen of God. Where shall Jesus begin? In a palace? No; for Jesus then, as now, loved a cottage. It is to be in a house where a carpenter's widow will be an honoured guest. The pearl of great price is independent of casket or setting, and needs not earthly splendour to make Him attractive. Where did Jesus begin? At Cana, near to home. It is a poor look-out when a man has to leave home to be popular. And if we have Jesus in our hearts, He will affect our home. He shall change dulness to brightness, and water to wine. We shall need true religion to be effective near to home. It is of no use talking of heavenly things to those who know what earth-worms we are. If we preach to those who know our lives are unworthy, they will bid us take a dose of our own physic. Where shall Jesus begin? At a funeral? No; a wedding. Some people can imagine Christ coming to comfort, but they cannot understand His coming to make glad. If we have Jesus at our amusements, He will not shun us in our grief. Ask Him to the wedding, and in the silence of the house where our dead lie in the darkened chamber, we shall hear Him whisper, "I will never leave thee, I will never forsake thee."

"*His disciples*" were asked.—And who have so much right at the wedding? Who have the same right to laugh and make merry as those whom Christ has chosen? The man who is going to heaven has a right to smile even when other men weep, and at a wedding he sees a parable. The bride is to share all her husband has, and the disciple remembers, that to be joined to Christ is to be a sharer of all the riches of God. The disciples were invited. Some men would like to have Christ, but not His Church. The Saviour, but not the saved. They are willing to meet them in heaven, but not in the same town. Will not such people feel a little ashamed in heaven; if they should ever come to the company of the firstborn?

There was *want at a wedding!*—That is not what we look for, but at Cana "they wanted wine." Perhaps Christ's disciples had increased in number before the wedding-day, but He took them all. Whenever God causes inconvenience He will Himself relieve us. We never need fear the embarrassment of success in the Lord's work. If He enlists more soldiers, He will find weapons and rations. Let our young readers mark, there was want at a wedding. Most young folks look forward to their marriage, that is, if they are the best kind of people for this world. Some people are so refined they do not care for such matters. However, we do not write for those who are more spiritual than the Bible. So let those who are looking forward to a nest of their own remember, that "settling" is not a synonym for marrying. It is most likely you may be more unsettled then than now. Life is the sphere of want. While you are in this world you will have to share its fortunes. The writer was in the Tower of London the other day, and saw the regalia of England. There were some splendid crowns, the diamonds and other jewels were a wondrous sight, and these were the Queen's; and yet the head-dress she wears mostly is not any of these jewelled diadems. The same day he looked into a print-shop window at the newest portrait of Her Majesty, and on her head was a widow's cap! Whatever else you have to leave out, be sure to have the love of God in your preparations for the wedding. Then Christ can make a crust delicious, and you may write on purse, cupboard, bookshelves, and even gravestone, "My God shall supply all your need."

At the beginning *Christ compelled Nature to take her proper place.*—It is well to do this at the beginning. Begin as you mean to hold out. The mother of Jesus was there. She had been used to rule her Son. His Father has owned Him. "This is *my* beloved Son," had been said; "henceforth it is meat and drink to do my Father's will." And so when Nature would control Grace, she is gently pushed on one side with, "What have I to do with thee?" Had the gentle Son confided to His mother the feelings of His heart, which told Him of wondrous popularity? and had the mother seen herself great in consequence? And now she is to be nothing! Was this the sword which was to pierce her heart? What is the natural tie as compared with the bond which makes one the whole of the believers in Jesus? "Whosoever shall do the will of God, the same is my brother and my sister and mother."

Let us see to it that Nature takes her place. If God asks for child, or gold, or time, or life, let not Nature keep them back. Duty, not pleasure, must be the mainspring of action. Conscience, not appetite, should steer. Nature may be allowed to find the sails. Loyalty to Christ must be the helm

Like Peter, who knew naturally all about fishing, but did not say, "Master, you are a carpenter, I am a fisherman, and am sure it is useless to go out now." No; he said, "Nevertheless at Thy word. Never mind that others will laugh me to scorn as they see me put out to sea. They have not heard Thee speak the word of command, and they will laugh very differently when I call them to come and help me store the fish." Let Nature wait, her hour will come. It is well for her when she is willing to fall behind, and whisper to the servants, brain and muscle, pen and sword, "Whatsoever He saith unto you, do it."

In studying Christ's conduct at the beginning, we may learn HOW TO WORK FOR GOD.—"*There were set there six water pots of stone.*" God uses that which is "set there." When He made man He did not take part of the materials of heaven: the dust of the ground was set there. And so Jesus did not send away for wine. When He wants channels of grace, He moulds them out of the earth. His missionaries are not angels, but men. Do not let us despise the vessels of His grace because they are familiar. Why should He not bless the pulpit in our church or chapel? Why should He not bless our own family altar? Why should He not call out of your class at Sunday-school some Moffat, or Hunt, or Martyn?

We should do well to imitate the servants. How willingly they worked. "Fill the water-pots with water." No question. No saying of—"Water at a wedding!" No fault-finding, but instant obedience. They filled them—and with more than obedience, enthusiasm—"to the brim." One of the wants of the Church is gleeful, enthusiastic service. One wonders to see men on 'change, and compare them when in church. The newspaper is conned as the Bible never is. Give us men and women who will obey Christ as the servants did, and the water of their poor talents shall be changed into the wine that shall make the whole world merry with delight in the goodness of God.

At the beginning Jesus taught us that HE KEEPS HIS BEST TO THE LAST.—At least, the governor said so, and he knew, for he tasted. How shall men judge Christ's wine without experience? "O taste, and see that the Lord is good." Why do we believe Satan? He knows nothing of redeeming love. It was the governor who praised the wine. It is a way governors have. Understrappers cannot afford to praise anything but themselves. The greater a man is, the more ready he is to appreciate greatness in others.

It is not Satan's plan to give the best last. He makes men drunk, and then gives them the dregs. There are numbers of men drinking at his table what they would not have looked at when they first sat down. If Absalom had known the end! If he could have seen himself lifted up, not on the throne, but on an oak, and if he could have seen Joab coming, not with a sceptre to put in his hand, but a dart to thrust into his heart, he would have said "No," and dashed the good wine to the ground.

Some of those who saw the beginning of miracles saw the end. They stood on Olivet, and watched their Lord as He was gently separated from them. They saw Him as He was slowly lifted; they watched His hands, still scarred, as they saw Him leaving them, but with a blessing. And when the heavens received Him, they would be ready to say to each other, "We saw the beginning of miracles, but it was nothing to this, 'Thou hast kept the good wine until now.'" Poor, tempted, harassed disciple, who hast so often feared for thyself, and art ready to halt at every step! Take courage, grace will be sweeter further on. Do not fear that thou wilt not succeed in reaching the good land. Though feeble, He can give thee strength to overcome. John Bunyan knew that, and so he tells us Miss Much-afraid "went through the river singing, but none could understand what she said." I trow they understood at the other side, and it would be,

"THOU HAST KEPT THE GOOD WINE UNTIL NOW!"

II.

THE GRANARY OF GOD.

GENESIS xliv. 1.

THIS is one of the many beautiful incidents in Joseph's life. His brethren have been feasted, and are now anxious to return. Their wives and children will soon be needing bread to save them from hunger; there must be no delay, and so, apparently in answer to their looks of uneasiness, rather than their words, the great man gives command. The *steward,*—how times change! He who a little time ago was a slave has now servants who haste to do his bidding; so many are they that he must have one at their head to take the orders from the master and see them carried out. "The whirligig of fortune brings its own revenge." Yes, he who was down yesterday is at the top to-day. The maligned and persecuted slave is now master of the land. He has no one to dispute his bidding. It did not look likely that one who was sent to jail for such a crime would ever be free again, but "God moves in a mysterious way His wonders to perform." Take comfort. If you are on the side of right, God will see that you are some day lifted into your right place. Have you been wrongfully accused? Your Master shall vindicate you sooner or later. Commit your reputation to Him, and if not before, the first time He has all the world together He will clear you. Everybody shall hear that you are right. One wonders what that vile wretch, Lady Potiphar, thought when she heard the trumpets proclaim Joseph the greatest of men. Most likely she was glad to eat the corn from Joseph's granaries. One would think it would almost choke her!

What a combination there had been, designed and undesigned, to keep God's favourite down. How the wheels fitted in each other, and cruel men and an unclean woman joined hand in hand to keep for baser use the fine gold! But 'tis all in vain that the wicked combine against the just. "Light is sown for the righteous." It is sometimes late in springing; but God's harvests are large ones, if far on in the autumn before gathered. They only linger to grow. Are you one of those who feel that you ought to rise in the world? Don't be afraid
The people want leaders, and if you are the right sort of stuff you will have a chance of going to the front sooner or later. Don't be sentimental, and whine about the "flowers that blush unseen." No combination can keep you down if you are a "rising" man. Never forget that he who had been sold as

a slave, lied against by a wicked woman, wrongfully imprisoned, lived to say to the steward of his house, "Fill the men's sacks with food," and the men were those who had sold him!

Joseph has always been a favourite type of Jesus. There is no wonder that it should be so. When we think of him, sent by his father, seeking his brethren, coming full of grace and truth to give them a blessing, while they are plotting his death, we are reminded of Him who "came unto His own, and His own received Him not." And in the generous treatment these brethren received at the hands of the man they had plotted against, we see a picture of the way Jesus treats those who had nailed Him to the tree. "Begin at Jerusalem." Joseph said, "Now therefore be not grieved, nor angry with yourselves, that ye sold me hither: for God did send me before you to preserve life." Jesus said in Jerusalem, by the mouth of His servant, "The people of Israel were gathered together for to do whatsoever Thy hand and Thy counsel determined before to be done." No wonder that in all ages the Church has loved to find in Joseph the foreshadowing of One who loved His brethren to the death.

"Fill the men's sacks with food!" It seems as though we heard our Joseph, exalted to be a Prince and a Saviour, saying to his stewards, the ministers and teachers of every sort, Fill with food, *not flowers*. It would have been worse than useless to have filled the sacks with specimens of the floral beauty of Egypt. Hungry men could not eat flowers, they cannot now; and yet some preachers act as though poetry and pretty ideas were the only things fit for food. Far better put a wreath of flowers round the ass's neck than put them in the sack where corn should be. It is said sometimes of these beautiful preachers when their hearers are asked, What was it about? what did he tell you?—"Ah, it was very beautiful, I was very much pleased, but somehow there was nothing to carry away!"

Food, not chaff!—Worse than even flowers, for they were pretty to look at before they faded, but dry, tasteless preaching, containing words without ideas, does not give pleasure, to say nothing of profit. What can men make of chaff? Of what use is mere verbiage? And yet, there are not a few who weary their hearers with their platitudes, and wonder that men sleep! Could men or children use their time better than in sleep, when preachers or Sunday School teachers speak what is but chaff, the shroud in which the living idea was, but now is not?

Food.—What preachers and teachers give their hearers has something to do with the character of their spiritual life. We cannot raise vigorous Christians on sour or insipid food, they will not eat enough of it; nor can we rear strong men on weak diet.

Let them have the finest of the wheat. It is in the granary, and only needs serving out. The mighty men of past generations of Christians were not fed with inferior food. The brave men and women who held fast the truth were fed on sound doctrine.

Fill.—Don't give them short measure. Full, pressed down, running over. There need be no stint. There is plenty. "My God shall supply all your need according to His riches." Why be afraid to let the people have all that God has promised? Fill every sack. Some of them are less than others. Let these be filled, whoever else may go short. The less the mind that comes, the more pains should be taken that it has a full sack. Let the thoughtless and the ignorant have special care. The others can fill for themselves, but these will only take what is given them. So let each have "as much as they can carry."

"Put their money in their sacks. I don't

want it. I don't sell corn to my brethren." Oh, how like our royal Joseph! He does not trade, He is a King. His grace is free. Salvation cannot be of grace and of debt! Do some of my readers feel they need food? Are their souls hungry? Come to Joseph. Do you tell me you have nothing to buy with? You are the most welcome. Capital is rather an hindrance than otherwise. It is enough for Him to see your hunger-bitten face, to make Him cry out, Fill him with what he needs. It is without money and without price. Money in their sacks. If they have any goodness, let them have the benefit. One who had been to the royal granary said, "My goodness extendeth not to thee, but to the saints that are in the earth." Take the money home with you. Let your wives and your children be the better for it.

As they set off with their laden sacks they remind us of many a congregation. There is old Mr. Faithful,—he has his sack full he has as much corn as he can carry. No wonder that he and his family do not want. He comes to the means of grace expecting to receive, and is not disappointed. But there is Mr. Incredulity: he looks, as usual, not very pleased with himself, or with anyone else. Well, what is the matter? You don't seem to have any corn. No, I did not think we should see the Master, I knew the steward was good for nothing, and so did not bring a sack. If I had known—— Ah, yes; but here comes Little Faith. Well, you have a bag full? Yes; but I have not as much as Faithful; you see he took a sack, and I had only a pillow slip. I might have done better. There, too, goes Miss Heedless. She has a sack, and it was filled, but there is a hole in the corner, and so the birds have a fine time. Still we may all sing—

> "So plenteous is the store,
> Enough for all, enough for each,
> Enough for evermore."

III.

THE FARMER'S GIFT.

2 KINGS iv. 42, 43.

THIS is a story worthy of an artist's pencil. It is a time of famine. There has been no rain, and hunger and want stare you in the face go where you will. The grass is all burned up, the trees look as though there had been a fire to dry up their sap, the leaves have fallen, and the branches are bare; the cattle and sheep are but living skeletons, and bleat and low for water, for the want of which they will die! How anxiety sits on the faces of all the men you see; even the man of God looks sorrowful, as he looks at the hunger-bitten faces of the sons of the prophets. Just after one of their number had nearly poisoned the rest by cooking some dangerous herb, they are cheered by the visit of a farmer, who comes with food which he intends for the prophet; but the old man will have his young friends share his fortune. Accordingly he bids his servitor give out the loaves and corn. What! Should I set this before a hundred men? He is told that he must obey, for God means the twenty small cakes and the few ears of corn to be a good meal for all those hungry men.

Here let me say to young men, *Don't be in a hurry to leave the old folks.* If these youngsters had said, as soon as their lesson was over, Come, we have had enough of the old fellow, let us be off to enjoy ourselves, they would have missed a good meal. If you will stay and be a comfort to those who have been at one time your only friends, they will appreciate your affection, and do their best to show it. If youth will linger near to age, it will share the last loaf.

There is in this little piece of Elisha's history A LESSON ON PROVIDENCE.

This dearth came in consequence of sin. The proud and wicked people would never yield, except they were obliged by God's strong hand. And when He punishes, He makes men know how powerful He is. Some men nowadays would not be touched in any other way. The writer remembers how, in the time of the cattle-plague, many ungodly farmers were forced to feel the hand of God, and just now we have had three or four bad harvests, so that many a godless man has felt, if this year is not better, he cannot pay his rent, but must be ruined. When God takes to preaching, His voice is heard outside the churches and chapels. The bad trade from which England is now suffering is to teach us, if we are not too stupid to learn, that if we will care for God's interests, and feed the hungry, and clothe the naked, instead of heaping such luxury on ourselves, He will bless us, but if not we shall see want at our own doors.

You cannot have retributive providences, and only the wicked suffer; the godly have their share of want. Elisha was in need. But the godly have some one to look up to. David said, "I have been young and now am old, yet have I not seen the righteous forsaken, nor his seed begging bread." Mark, he does not say that it never happened, but that in his long life he had not seen it. We often forget that God is as strong now as ever He was. The God of to-day is the God of the Old Testament:—the manna God,—the barrel of meal God,—the God who has said, "Call upon me in the day of trouble and I will deliver thee." If God had once broken His word, and allowed one of those who trusted on Him to be disappointed, His enemy would have made the world to know it. Only let God forsake one who puts his trust in Him, and Satan would put the name and address in "the agony column" of the *Times*. But we feel sure he will never need use his money for that kind of advertisement!

There is here A BEAUTIFUL EXAMPLE OF BENEVOLENCE. We don't know the farmer's name who relieved the prophet. He was one of a noble band of nameless ones, but some day God will publish a report, and we shall find his name, and if we don't live to see that book, we may go to heaven, and Elisha will gladly introduce his friend to us. We know where he came from,—the village has got into the Bible, through the man's goodness. It is possible to make our birthplace famous by living for Jesus. We sometimes say, he gives twice who gives quickly. The farmer gave as soon as he could. There

27, PATERNOSTER ROW, LONDON.

... AND STOUGHTON'S
PUBLICATIONS.

...NLOW NORTH;
...AND RECOLLECTIONS
BY THE REV.
... *MOODY STUART, M.A.*

... 8vo, cloth, price 7s. 6d.

... of this well-known Evangelist con...
... of his earlier years, a narrative of ...
... a review of the substance and char...
... titles of the chapters are :—

... Earlier Years.
... Conversion.
... Efforts to Win Souls.
... ...istic Work.
...
... ...tion as an Evangelist by the Free Ch...
...
... North's Post-bag.
... ...orth's Portfolio.
... ...ndrew North's Theology ; comprisin...

... and Personality of God.
... ...ration of Scripture.
... ...ality of the Soul.
... ... Birth.
... ...tion by Faith not Feeling.

... ...hood and in London.
... ... in various Fields.
... ...ses of Conversion.
... ...tracts from his Annotated Bibles.
...
... ...stolic Labours.
... Labour in Glasgow.
... by Personal Friends.
... Rest.

seems to have been a little rain that fell on his field, and the barley had come up; so, as soon as he could, he threshed it, and said to the wife, Do be quick and bake me a few cakes to take to the prophet. "Bread of the first fruits," we are told it was. Don't wait till you have churned, and give God the butter-milk. For many wait to be rich before they will be generous, only to find that their heart is too sour to give anything. First fruits! Young men, do not wait till the candle of your life is burned to the socket, and offer Him but the snuff. Give God the best part of your life, that which has the sunshine. If you will care for God with your May and June, He will care for you in November.

He came himself. He did not send it. If you want a thing well done do it yourself. Especially is this true of acts of benevolence. Be your own *almoner*. "Pure religion and undefiled before God the

Father is to visit the fatherless and widow." Visit them does not mean that you are to be content with putting a shilling in the box at the time of the communion. Nor does it mean that you give the money to your minister to give for you. Go yourself up the narrow stair, lift the latch, let the poor have the luxury of a quarter of an hour of your company. Some of the poor are rich in faith, and we shall be glad of a call from them when they are in the mansion which God is furnishing so splendidly for them.

This farmer *increased God's capital.* The rule is, that God works by means. He does not usually act without the assistance of His creatures. Many of His plans are unfinished because the men are on strike! Let it be said, with all reverence, this miracle could not have been performed if the man had not come from Baalshalisha with the corn and cakes. The prophet might have been fed, but not in this way. This opens up a wide subject. It is worth our while to ask, Can we increase the revenue of God? Is there another half-hour we can spend in His service? Can we find out any other way of usefulness? Would it not be better to let the Saviour have the benefit of the legacy duty by giving the money while we are yet in the world?

The good farmer ACCOMPLISHED A GREAT DEAL MORE THAN HE INTENDED. He meant feeding the prophet, and he fed a hundred others! And is not this the case now-a-days? When Robert Raikes began his Sunday-school he only thought of the poor ignorant children of Gloucester; he little thought that he would be imitated, and that there would be thousands of Sunday-schools. When Charles Wesley asked Böhler if he must tell of his joy in Christ, the answer was, "If you had a thousand tongues, tell it with them all." He little thought that the idea would be set to rhyme, but Wesley wrote,—

> "O for a thousand tongues to sing
> My great Redeemer's praise!"

and that has been sung by millions of happy Christians in all parts of the world. The fact is, God can make a much better use of our talents than any one else can. You cannot get so much interest for your money anywhere else. Lord Byron was a much greater poet than Isaac Watts, but they will be singing Watts' hymns when Byron's name is forgotten.

Elisha would not have had the chance of feeding his students if the farmer had not brought the corn. And the good man was equal to his opportunities. In spite of the sneer of his wretched servitor, who was then in training for leprosy, he would have the cakes divided. "Give unto the people that they may eat." How like God! He does not sell, but gives, and so it is with the bread of life. It is given to whoever will come. Are you hungry? Does your soul need satisfying? His mercy can do it. Accept the spiritual food offered to you. "*They did eat,*" we read; and it is not enough for you to hear of Christ;—believe,—rest. Do with salvation as the hungry student did with the cakes. Appropriate it. Do not be afraid. There is plenty more.

"Enough in Christ remains behind
To fill the souls of all mankind."

It would be difficult to say who was the happiest in the group, Elisha or the farmer. It was not Gehazi. It must have been very interesting to hear the good man describe what he had seen. Can you not fancy him when he reaches the farm? The wife, anxious to know how the prophet had liked her cakes, says, "Well, my dear, and did you find the prophet?" "Find him: I should think I did, my lass; I never had such a day in my life. What do you think? When I got there, I saw more than a hundred of the young men, and fine fellows they are, but they did look poor. I wished I had taken ten times as much. But I need not have done. When the good prophet saw me, he cried out, 'Gehazi, take these cakes and the corn to the students.' He's a greedy one, is that servant man! He said, 'What use are these few little cakes to set before all these hungry men?' 'Do as I tell you,' says Elisha. 'The Lord says they shall eat, and shall leave.' You would not believe it, but all those hungry men ate, and yet they could not eat all my cakes! Elisha said, 'Eat away;' they did their best, but they had to leave. They *did* eat, but, hungry as they were, they 'left thereof according to the word of the Lord.'"

IV.

THE HOLY TENT.

"Let them make me a sanctuary, that I may dwell among them."—EXODUS xxv. 8.

HOW easily God could have made the tabernacle Himself! Then everything would have been perfect,—the precious stones, the gold, the embroidery, how beautiful if He had but shown us what He could do! Yes, but it would not have given Him the pleasure it did. "My delights were with the sons of men." Perhaps some of us are wearing a watchchain made out of hair. We could have bought a better one, that would have looked more handsome, but this is worth more to us than any other. It was made by the fingers of our child, made for our birthday. In some such way, God delights in that which His children do for Him. It would be easier to send out angels to do the preaching, but it must be an intense delight to our God and Saviour to see men toiling to find ideas which shall strike their hearers, and lead them to truth and salvation; and especially to see a young man working hard to master the difficulties of some foreign tongue, that he may tell the story of the cross to the heathen. It does not take a vivid imagination to picture God listening to the axe as it cuts down trees for the posts of the tabernacle, and that dull chopping would sound as musical to Him as the angel's song. But there is no charm in what is not done for God with a free heart. "*Of every man that giveth willingly with his heart* ye shall take my offering."

We should mark that GOD MAKES HIMSELF DEPENDENT ON THE WILL OF MAN.—

"Let them make me." This is true, not only of material wealth, but of man's nature. God wants human nature, He seems to covet to have the affection of our life, and yearns to be looked up to by the creature He has made. Let us not cheat Him, for we shall rob ourselves most of all. There are two passages of Scripture which we will place together: "Who will have all men to be saved;" "Ye will not come unto me." What mystery in these words! Who can tell us all we could ask concerning them? But one thing is plain, God may be thwarted by man.

Was not the holy tent a picture of the Church? Built, not in Egypt, but in the wilderness, and built that God might dwell among men. Does not Paul use the same idea, when writing to the people of Corinth, "Ye are the temple of the living God, as God hath said, I will dwell with them. Wherefore come out from among them, and be ye separate?" and is not the tent of God a shadow of the perfect Church we read of at the end of the Book? "Behold, the tabernacle of God is with men, and He will dwell among them." Was not this in the mind of the man who wrote the child's hymn in which these lines occur?—

> "I have been there and still would go,
> *'Tis like a little heaven below.*"

In this divine conception of the Church THERE IS A PLACE FOR THE RICH. It is not impossible for rich men to be good men. It is not easy, but still it can be done. It is foolish to sneer at the givings of the rich. God has given them a place. This is the offering which ye shall take of them— "*gold.*" None but He who reads the heart, knows what sacrifices many of the rich make in giving gold. Do you reply, they do not give in proportion to the poor? No, but the poor do not feel giving like the wealthy do. It is much more easy out of the little to give a little, than to give in the same proportion out of the much. The writer knows a man who spent £30,000 on his pictures, and who gives at the rate of £100 per annum to the support of the ministry; but he says he cannot go on giving at that rate. Why? It does not give him the pleasure the pictures do! It is only for the Lord, not for himself. God would not have accepted planks from those who had gold, and so God will not accept industry in His service in the place of wealth. However well the rich man can teach in the Sunday-school, it must not be put in the place of the material wealth he can put into God's hands.

LABOUR HAS ITS PLACE.—There was a great deal of timber required; the wood of the acacia-tree was used for the framework. What a number of trees would have to be cut down; perhaps many miles walked before one is found large enough; then the axe must be plied,—these boards mean thousands of drops of sweat. When the tree was cut down, it had to be sawn into boards, and other shaped timbers; then there was the labour of dragging them to the place where the tabernacle was put together. Here was work which the poorest could do. It was well when the man who had given gold or silver took his axe, and was a hewer of wood; but you could not shut the poor man out,—he had his chance of "giving willingly with his heart" the toil which was his talent. Is it not so to-day? In building the Church, what room for holy industry! Ply thy axe and saw, my brother. The gold of the rich is useless without the toil of thy hands. The plates of gold were to cover the boards of acacia. Gold would not do of itself; it was the ornamental, rather than the useful. And what would the missionary income of the

Churches be without the missionaries? Fancy the Missionary Societies if no one offered for the work. If, as each man died, or came home, no one went out, what a difference it would make! Does some mother read this? Has she a boy who sometimes talks as though he would be a missionary if his way were open? Give him to the Lord. You may only be able to put a penny into the collection, but if you have given a man for the work, we shall want other signs beside £ s d to tell the worth of your offering.

WOMAN HAS HER RIGHTS HERE.—We read in Exodus xxxv. 24, 25 of women that were wise-hearted, who did spin with their hands, and of "women whose heart stirred them up in wisdom spun goats' hair." If we take woman's work out of the Church, what a great many good labourers we lose at once. Think of the influence of all the Christian mothers: who can reckon it? Think of the devoted Sunday-school workers among the women; think of the thousands of tracts given by women's hands. Think of the mothers' meetings. Women have their work in the Church, and no one can take their place. Then let the woman do her work well. If it is for you to spin, do it with wisdom. Let not the enemy whisper that your work is such a feeble contribution. God did not expect the woman to cut down the trees; there is a place, and a right place, for us all. A manly woman is as much out of place as an effeminate man. We don't like to see the woman shoulder the axe, no more than the man finger distaff and spindle. Still we are not independent of the woman; we must have her work, or we cannot finish ours. Paul was every whit a man, and he never flinched from his duty, but he could appreciate the work of the other sex, and has given her a place of beauty in his letters, "These women which laboured with me in the gospel."

THERE IS ROOM FOR GENIUS.—Not only gold, silver, brass, and wood, but *precious stones* are required; the beautiful jewels worn by the high priest were considered as part of the furnishing of the tabernacle. Of course the onyx stones, and other jewels, took up but small room, but they added beauty and splendour to the rest. God does not create genius every day. We have many rhymers, but few poets, and small indeed is the proportion of these who write hymns. If Byron had written a "Christian Year," that is, if he had been as devout as Keble, what a different book it would have been! We need the ruby as well as the pearl. How little does painting help the truth nowadays. Look at our railway stations. If those great spaces could be utilized for God as the painters in olden time would have used them, what room for large frescoes, what teaching through the eye! Let the reader cast his eye on the hoardings, and see the advertisements, so pictorial and striking, and not an inch of them used for Jesus or teaching truth and righteousness. The tabernacle is inhabited by God, though not adorned as it deserves; would it not give Him pleasure if He could have the kind of beauty only possible for genius to produce?

Still, we must not forget that the MEANEST IS ACCEPTABLE, IF IT IS THE BEST WE CAN BRING.—Cedar for Solomon's temple, Shittim wood for the tabernacle, for even Solomon could not have provided cedar where the holy tent was made. There are times when cleverness is baffled, and wealth is powerless. Our best is welcome, however inferior it may be to someone else's best. God does not reap where He has not sown, though the indolent servant made it out to be so. But see to it God has your best. Let us not pray in the stead of working. There are those who can shout "Thy kingdom come" easier than they can try to bring it about. Acacia-wood will not be accepted in the place of anything else. But if the axe and saw are your talents, by all means use them. If we could only have the buried one talent, we should have a wonderful increase to the Church's revenues. The four men who carried the paralytic could not heal him, but they could take off the tiles; and to such workers Jesus cannot say nay. When He saw their eager faces looking through the hole they had made in the roof, He could not deny them the pleasure of seeing their friend rise and take up his bed.

OUR BEST AND OUR ALL IS OF NO AVAIL WITHOUT THE ATONEMENT.—We read, in Hebrews ix. 21, "Moreover, he sprinkled likewise with blood, both the tabernacle and all the vessels of the ministry." Besides, the foundations of the tent were silver blocks, which were bought with the redemption shekels. Every man was redeemed, and the price was that on which the framework rested (Exodus xxx. 16, and xxxviii. 27). " This habitation of God" rests on the true foundation which is Christ Jesus. Let none of us rest upon our alms or deeds; they are, though precious and beautiful, only safe as they rest upon the merits of Jesus.

> "Not the alms or works of man
> Can for his sins atone,
> But the Lamb for sinners slain
> Hath satisfied alone."

V.

THE HOLY CHEST.

HEBREWS ix. 4.

"OF which we cannot now speak particularly," said the author of this epistle. If he had gone into particulars, further exposition would have been needless. What was the lesson taught by this wonderful article of tabernacle furniture? Are we not to look upon it as a picture of Jesus? If the reader does not think so, let him, like the Bereans, "search the scriptures, whether these things were so."

Let us consider the OUTSIDE. What do we see? a chest most likely about three feet long, by eighteen inches wide, and eighteen inches deep. It is a box made of common wood, but covered with fine gold; and is not our Jesus both human and divine? Both are there, and you cannot separate them; just as the ark was not perfect, though the right shape and size, till it was covered with fine gold, so Christ could not be Jesus without the gold of divinity. The Jews stumbled here; they were ready to receive a human Messiah, but they would not have anything to do with the divine element. We, however, have been better taught, and look for One anointed to save. Still we do not overlook the wood, though it is covered with gold. It is sweet to know that Christ shares our nature. He passed over the cedar of angelic life, and took the common shittim, the tree of the wilderness. When we think of our sins, we are thankful that our Saviour was divine, and therefore able to save to the uttermost; but when we think of our future, we are glad that we are to spend our eternity with the *Man* Christ Jesus. He is one of ourselves. "It behoved Him to be made like unto His brethren."

Do you notice that at each corner there is a ring of gold? What are these rings for? To receive the staves which are passed through the rings. By these gold-covered staves the Levites carried the ark on their shoulders. The holy thing was portable; it went before, and led the people on their march. They were sure to be safe if they went where the ark led them. It would be a blessed thing if the Church of God would be persuaded to go only where Christ would have gone. They would be saved from much temptation; not that God would have us morose and unfit for company. Jesus loved society; He delighted to sit down at the table with His friends, and to accept hospitality; yet He would not have gone where some of His so-called followers show themselves.

But what are these figures which stand at each end of the ark,—winged creatures,

THE HOLY CHEST. 47

whose faces are looking with such earnestness at the gold on the top of the ark? These are the cherubim, the representatives of the angelic world. They gaze with interest upon the mercy-seat. Is it not Jesus who links heaven to earth? We sometimes wonder what angels are like, and how it is that they who never knew pain or sorrow should be so much interested in this world of transgression and tears. We read, "which things the angels desire to look into." How powerful these beings are; one of them slew thousands in one night: how pure they are; they have never broken the law. What an advantage it will be for us to mix with them, and to spend eternity in their company; and this will be the case, for, in Him whom the ark pictured, "the whole family in heaven and earth is named."

Upon what are the cherubim gazing so intently? Follow the direction of their eyes, and what see you? *There is a spot of blood!*

Blood? Yes, blood. Blood on the pure gold? Yes, this ark is the meeting-place between God and man,—the only place where the Holy God can be approached by him who represents sinners. The Socinian sneers at us for talking so much about blood. He is so refined that he cannot bear such things. Nay, he is more refined than the Almighty, for God commanded that whenever the high priest approached the mercy-seat, he should bring blood with him (see Lev. xvi. 14). Just as the cherubim gazed upon the blood which was sprinkled on the gold, so in heaven, to-day, the Saviour is the centre of attraction, and not as the King of glory, but as a newly-slain victim—"a Lamb as it had been slain." And if the reader ever stands with those who sing the song of Moses and the Lamb, he must come to the mercy-seat, to the appointed place for pardon. Have you been there? If not, come at once. Come and look at the blood which is on the gold. That blood of the Innocent was shed for thee. Thou need'st not fear to meet God in the place He has appointed to look upon the sinner. Gaze upon the ark,—the wood, the gold, the blood,—which is the sacrifice for thy sins, and then thou shalt be able to sing :—

> "Thou standest in the holy place,
>   As now for guilty sinners slain,
>   The blood of sprinkling speaks and prays,
>   All prevalent for guilty men.
>   Thy blood is still my ransom found,
>   And speaks salvation all around."

We will now lift the lid of the ark and look INSIDE. What do we see? "*The golden pot.*" A vessel of gold filled with manna! God commanded that a pot of manna should be placed in the ark. Some of the angels' food was picked up from the ground and preserved. There it is, not breeding worms, as all other manna did if kept, but fresh as the first day it was gathered. Does not this teach that in Christ we have spiritual food?

Just as the manna fell all the time the children of Israel were in the wilderness, so Jesus is the bread of life to us, all the time we are on this side Jordan. We shall need the Saviour as long as we are in this sinful world. There is a time coming when we shall hunger no more, but, till then, it is our safety to eat the "bread which came down from heaven."

Have another peep inside, and what meets your gaze? *The rod that budded* (Numb. xvii.). Do you remember the story? There had been a rebellion; Korah, Dathan, and Abiram had tried to show that they had as much right to be priest as Aaron. They had been swallowed up, and the next day Moses told the princes to bring their sceptres; each tribe was thus represented. Aaron's name was written on the rod of Levi. They were all laid before the Lord. The next day they were all brought out, and lo, Aaron's rod had received life and bore a crop of almonds as well as blossom! It was a mass of flowers and fruit. By this the people were convinced that Aaron was chosen to be priest, and the rod was kept in the ark. What does this teach us? That in Christ is the true, God-chosen, God-honoured, God-prevalent priesthood.

We have numbers of sham priests. There is the priest of idolatry: his sceptre is but a blood-stained club. There was the Jewish priest, but he is a dry stick, there is no life there: all barrenness. There is the Romish priest, but this is a rotten stick; we despair of seeing it bloom with anything but religious fungus. Away with all these shams! Christ is the true priest, and we feel that in Christ we have all we need.

> "He entered once the holiest,
> And therefore I shall enter,
> Who Jesus own,
> On Him alone
> For full salvation venture;

> The earnest and the witness,
> And seal of sins forgiven,
> He bought for me—
> With purity,
> And all the joys of heaven."

Look again. What see you now? "*The tables of the covenant.*" The stones upon which God wrote the law. Not the first tables: they were broken. Moses did not pick up the fragments and patch them together and put them in the ark. No, it was the new, unbroken tables, which were put in the ark. And is not Christ Jesus our righteousness? Do we not glory in the fact that our Substitute was sinless? We have no righteousness to plead, but we have a perfect Saviour. Our efforts at reformation are but a clumsy piecing of the broken tables, but in Christ we have a perfect law. The blood of the covenant is what we rejoice over. *Innocent blood on an unbroken law!*

It would be an interesting theme to dwell upon—*the history of the ark.* How it was bound up with the success of the friends of God. Wherever it went, it meant destruction to the foes of the Almighty. When Jericho was to be taken, the ark of the Lord was carried round the doomed city. Nothing could stand before it. Perhaps some of my readers may remind me of the time when the ark was taken by the Philistines. Yes, but God had no greater foes that day than the men who carried the ark to the battle (Sam. iv. 4). They would not have been in the battle but for the ark which took them to death! The enemies of God had but scant cause for triumph. Dagon was cast down before the ark, and the plagues which came made the Philistines more glad to see the last of the ark than they had been to secure it. Yes, our success is here. If Jesus be with us, we shall win the day. If He is not in our place, we fail. Rams' horns, with the ark, do more than silver trumpets without it.

And in the last great struggle, when we cross the dark, bridgeless river, we shall need Christ, and if He is with us, all is well. Jordan was on a flood the day the Israelites crossed to the land of promise. What was to be done? The ark was brought, and as the priests' feet touched the swift stream the waters divided, and there was a passage for all,—old and young, the strong and the weak, the active youth and the lame man on his crutches, all passed over. Not till the last of the chosen ones had crossed, was the ark removed. And so now, our Jesus keeps the way. Fear not, poor pilgrim, for as thou passest over, louder than the roar of the torrent thou shalt hear a voice from the ark saying,—

"They shall not overflow thee."

VI.

THE TEMPTATION.

MATTHEW iv. 1-11.

SOMEWHERE or other the writer has seen a picture of the Iron Duke revisiting Waterloo. There sits Wellington on horseback, looking over the field where he won the most decisive of modern battles, and close by stands a guide, pointing out the most interesting parts of the field, little guessing to whom he is speaking, and how much better the listener could tell the story if he cared to do so.

Do we not at times, when listening to preachers talking of Christ's works and words, wonder whether they ever think that He stands by, and must be ready to smile at the blunders made by even his greatest admirers?

The temptation of Christ is a subject to excite the imagination, and tempt one to talk when it would perhaps be wiser to wait till we are with Jesus, when we can do as His disciples were wont when on earth,—ask Him privately. It becomes such as we are, to say, as we think of the wondrous struggle between Light and darkness, "Let the words of my mouth, and the meditation of my heart, be acceptable in Thy sight, O Lord, my Strength and my Redeemer."

One cannot help thinking and wondering why this temptation should take place, and though all the reasons cannot be known, some of them we think we can see. WE KNOW THERE IS A DEVIL. Perhaps the most clever of all Satanic schemes is that in which he persuades men that he does not exist. What could suit a general better than to persuade the troops he is seeking to destroy, that he is a mere creature of the imagination?—that all the stories told about him being seen are mere inventions, and that therefore there is no need to take any precautions? If we receive the Gospels as history, we must believe in a personal devil. Read Matthew iv. 11; and if you don't believe in the existence of the devil, you must become a Sadducee at once. If no bad spirit, neither are there good ones. If there was no temptation, there was no ministering. Where shall we stop when once we change the narrative into fable? Was the baptism a myth? If not, we must go on with the story, and accept the temptation as true, and believe there is, in spite of what clever men, taught by the father of lies, say, such an one as is called "that old serpent the devil."

If Christ had not been tempted, we should have heard the old mocking laugh of Satan, as when God spoke of Job, "Thou hast set a hedge about him." If Satan had not been worsted in the struggle, how cleverly would he have insinuated that the Saviour was not perfect! "If I had been allowed my way, I would have proved the second Adam no better than the first. I would soon have brought him down to the same level as the rest of the children of men." Have you ever stood on the beach when a new lifeboat has been tried? If so, you will have noticed that, not waiting till there is a storm abroad, and a wreck needing help, but some fine day, the boat is manned, and when out in deep water the crew capsize her, only to prove that she can right herself, and that there is no need to fear that she cannot live in the roughest sea. But the lifeboat built to save the wrecked world was tried as soon as launched, only to prove that the wildest storm could not capsize her, and that to be aboard was to reach the shore unhurt! SATAN CANNOT SAY CHRIST IS UNTRIED.

Then, it has been proved that A MAN CAN RESIST SIN in its strongest forms, for it was not as God that Jesus was tempted, but as the Son of man. It was the human nature that was tempted. Where would be the force of the reasoning in Hebrews iv. 15, if we are to believe that it was the divine and not the human which fought and won the battle? "*Like as we are.*" It was not possible for the divine in Jesus to learn anything, but it was possible for the human to do so, and so "*learned He obedience by the things which He suffered.*" It is these things which make us thankful to the Holy Ghost, who foreknew all the future of the human race, that He led Jesus into the wilderness to be tempted of the devil.

As we read the story of the temptation, we cannot but be struck with the ignorance of Satan concerning Jesus. He did not understand Him. There could be no doubt that He was a man; everything about Him was human,—He is hungry like any other man, and though He has fasted forty days, it is only what other good men have done; and if he could draw Moses into speaking unadvisedly, meek as he was, why should he not entrap this one? We know that he could not, but we should not have known it as we know it now, if Satan had not made the attempt. Let us not lose sight of the fact that the arch enemy is not omniscient. He learns quickly, but there are many things he has yet to learn. He is as ignorant as we are concerning the future, and fluent as he is in quoting Scripture, he is so blinded by prejudice that his eyes are holden. Besides, he, like bad men, is ready to think that every one is as bad as himself. Let us not be discouraged, then, if he treats us as though we were the vilest of men. How often have the purest-minded to stop their ears, and to cry out for help because tempted to that from which their minds start back

THE TEMPTATION. 61

with horror. The fact is, Satan cannot appreciate goodness, and makes as many mistakes as ever. How totally ignorant of Jesus he must have been to say, "All these things will I give thee, if thou wilt fall down and worship me." Be not surprised then if you are horrified by being solicited to do that from which your soul recoils. "The servant is not above his Lord," and if Jesus was asked to worship the devil, we must expect to be humiliated, if we cannot be overpowered by the suggestions of the Evil One.

How powerless temptation was when urged upon Jesus! There was no sympathy between the two. What concord hath Christ with Belial? Fire and water might be expected to agree, before Jesus and the devil could possibly come to terms. There was nothing in Jesus to respond to temptation. "Nothing in me," said the Lord, three years afterwards, when speaking of the last assault of the enemy. Why should not we know more of this experience? "Christ in you the hope of glory" is the power that can turn the alien army back. And where is the limit of this "Christ in you" power? The mistake which many of us make is supposing that it is necessary that we should be smitten down at every attack of the enemy. What the Church needs is more of "Christ in you." The self-denying power that makes men seek their happiness in wiping away tears from other faces, even at the cost of tears in their own eyes, is the kind of strength that makes human nature impregnable.

Jesus has taught us the use of the Bible in self-defence. The Captain of our salvation girded Himself with the Sword of the Spirit. He has showed us how to use it, and, what is remarkable, each quotation is from a part of Holy Writ that foes and false friends have alike agreed to discredit, The Pentateuch. Have my readers learned

THE TEMPTATION. 63

the sword exercise? It is useless to expect to conquer without the heavenly brand. You will be mortally wounded if you are not able to parry the strokes of the enemy. We never leave our home without our sword but Satan knows. Dust on the Bible lids invites the foe to make another attack. Courage is not enough. Like Jesus, let us have skill in applying the word of God to the temptations of the evil one. Search out the meaning of God's word, and what you know, use. There was great vehemence in the words of Jesus. He was not content to parry the stroke; He cut with the edge of His blade. And the wounds He made have not healed to this day!

The battle, though fierce, is not for ever. We read, "Then the devil leaveth Him." So it is with all the tempted followers of Jesus. Satan is not able to continue always. Sooner or later he must leave. Angels came. Evil first. Trial first. Sufferings first; then rest and quietness. "Through fire and water into a wealthy place." The sweet follows the bitter. What was true of the Master shall be true of all His servants. The devil will do his worst, only to be beaten, and then, angels come. And the same ears that heard Apollyon say, "I swear by my infernal den that thou shalt go no further; here will I spill thy soul," shall hear the shining ones say, as they go over the river, "We are ministering spirits, sent forth to minister for those that shall be heirs of salvation." "Now you must know that the city stood upon a mighty hill; but the pilgrims went up that hill with ease, because they had these two men to lead them up by the arms; also they had left their mortal garments behind them in the river, for though they went in with them, they came out without them. They therefore went up through the regions of the air, sweetly talking as they went, being comforted because they safely got over the river, and had such glorious companions to attend them." "The servant shall be as his Lord," and it shall be said of each of God's people as it was of Jesus,—"Then the devil leaveth Him, and behold, angels came and ministered unto Him."

> "Lost by the first, the second Man
> Jehovah did the fight regain,
> Single he foil'd our hellish foe,
> Who fled to escape the deadly blow.
> Nor could the serpent save his head
> For ever crushed—when Jesus bled!"

VII.

WINNING GOD'S BATTLES.

"And Joshua discomfited Amalek with the edge of the sword."—EXODUS xvii. 13.

THIS is a bulletin, not a gazette. We are used to see the general's name in the hasty statement sent off immediately after the victory, but, when the successful leader pens his gazette, he particularises, and gives the details of the battle, which regiments distinguished themselves, and even names individuals who have won honour by their acts of bravery, so that we now know, not merely the victor's name, but the more humble names of those who helped him to win, and we learn that he "begs to recommend Private Smith for the Victoria Cross."

Some day, our Joshua shall slay Amalek utterly. The last battle shall be won, and evil rear its ugly head no more. Then, when the books are opened, every good deed shall be read out, and secret acts of bravery and goodness shall be honoured. There are not a few, who have been unknown to fame, who will shine as the stars for ever and ever.

We learn from Deuteronomy xxv. 18 that Amalek had "smote the hindmost, even all that were feeble." In the presence of the enemy there should be no stragglers. These are always a temptation to the foe. Let us never forget that when we are feeble or straggling we are a mark for the enemy. Do you think no one knows when we are living far from God? Is the maid who dusts our bedroom the only one who looks on the Bible lids, and could write our names in the dust? When we absent ourselves from the Ordinance of the Lord's Supper, is the minister the only one who detects our absence? Be sure of this: when the enemy sees you leave your home without prayer, he sends word before you, and there are new temptations awaiting you in business. The hindmost, and the feeble, are sure to be the first attacked, and therefore should have special care. Amalek hangs about the flank; so let there be a rear guard of picked soldiers to care for what the writer of the Epistle to the Hebrews calls "the feeble knees, and the hands which hang down."

Joshua discomfited AMALEK, not Moses or some other friend. There are plenty of enemies, without fighting our brethren. What sport it must be for the alien when he sees the soldiers of the cross wounding each other! Whatever we men may think of the volumes of controversial divinity, the reading of them must have made laughter for the foe who hates both sides. For instance, good John Wesley stayed at home to write those pithy and drastic pamphlets against Toplady and Hill, while the good work of saving men from hell had to pause. And then Toplady must leave the composing of such hymns as "Rock of Ages," and pen a rejoinder that would make Wesley feel as though some one had cast vitriol upon him! If we are wounded fighting Amalek, it will not increase our pension, for we shall be too ashamed of the wounds we receive in battling with brethren to say anything about them. Let us keep our bitterness for sin, and our swords for the King's enemies. We are soldiers, and not gladiators; so, while there is an enemy of Christ left, we had better spend all our strength and courage in battling for the Lord, and not in wounding each other.

Amalek is not to be beaten without A FIGHT. This is no review. It is not work for blank cartridge. The struggle against sin is real, as we shall find to our cost if we are not wary. How Satan must laugh and sneer at many of the efforts made against him: sermons preached without point, Sunday-school lessons and addresses with no interest or teaching in them. We must come to close quarters. Mere commonplace generalities are not enough. It is not long-pounders, but the sword, that wins the day. When a young Spartan complained to his mother that his sword was too short, he was told to go a step nearer the enemy, and it would be long enough then.

Let us not forget to use the *edge* of the sword. Neither the flat of it nor the back will cut as a sword ought. There was a picture in one of the illustrated papers the other day of some Turks at the grindstone, getting their swords ready for the fight. What sort of an edge has yours? Has it an edge at all? All other things being equal, God can do more with a sharp man than a dull one. Don't be afraid of study, or anything else that will make you more effective.

Few things are so much to be dreaded as respectable dulness!

Moses was for EACH MINDING HIS OWN WORK—Joshua to fight, and himself to take the top of the hill. This is the way battles are won. The Commissariat officer serves his country while securing bullocks for rations, and sending up ammunition to the front. There is, perhaps, not enough thought of those who supply the wants of the workers. Have you ever noticed, at a fire, how all attention is given to the engine when it comes up, laden with men, who spring off, each one running to his post, some fixing on the hose, some getting out ladders, while another with the brazen pipe goes to the place of danger, and battles with the fire? There is another man at work, though, whom no one cares to look at. The turncock, with his large key, has gone down a back street, where there is no admiring crowd, and he turns on the water, without which the brave firemen would be of no use, and the mob would have nothing to cheer at. Is it not so with some unobtrusive men and women who find the funds for carrying on the work which others do? Let us not undervalue *any* kind of work, whether it is done publicly or in secret, knowing that the Master will "give every man according as his work shall be." This battle would not have been fought, to say nothing of won, if there had not been GOOD ADVICE given and taken. "Moses said unto Joshua." "Joshua did as Moses had said." What is the use of experience, if it does not speak? Why wait till your advice is asked? Why has God kept you in the world, old man, if He may not have the benefit of your experience? Don't wait till the chance has gone by, and then say, "Ah, I knew it would be so!" And if Moses speaks to Joshua, let not the young chief think that the old fogey is always interfering. It is not for nothing that God keeps the grey head here, instead of taking it home to be crowned.

"CHOOSE us out men," said Moses. Don't take *any* fool. There is a standard in the Queen's army. Each man must pass the doctor. It is not everybody who can be even a raw recruit. Are we particular enough about our soldiers in the army of the Lord? Do we not set men over the house of God who have not brains enough to take charge of anything else? We should fight all the better if we had better officers, even if there were fewer of them. Oh, if we could but secure for the army of God the same amount of bravery and generalship there is on the wrong side!

Moses on the hill is AN EMBLEM OF PUBLIC PRAYER. On the top of the hill, where all the fighting men could see him. Would you not like to have heard the prayer Moses put up that day? He was a wonderful man to pray. He who could say, " Blot my name out of Thy book," would be sure to offer a remarkable prayer when he saw his countrymen beloved attacked by Amalek. It was a prayer that remembered the past. He took the rod of God in his hand. What a history that rod had. It was the old shepherd's crook that Moses used in Midian. Before the Lord it had been changed into a serpent. It had beckoned to the waves of the Red Sea, and they had divided, and made a path for the Israelites to pass over, and again had been waved over the waters, and the floods returned to their place, drowning the enemies of God. It had smitten the rock in Horeb, and there had been water for the people to drink; and now Moses takes it with him to the top of the hill. Do we not forget too often the things God has honoured in the past? Where God honours, let us not show neglect, but continue to keep in hand that which "smote Rahab and wounded the dragon."

There is a mystery about prayer that we cannot unravel. How it is, or why it is, that success in the highest sense is more or less dependent upon the prayers of others than the worker, is a puzzle; but facts in spiritual, as well as natural life, are stubborn things. "This kind goeth not out but by prayer and fasting," was not spoken by some enthusiastic scholar, but by the Great Master Himself. The fact is plain enough, though the why and wherefore are kept secret. We have here the history, if not the philosophy, of success, or the want of it. *"And it came to pass, when Moses held up his hand, that Israel prevailed, and when he let down his hand Amalek prevailed."* Could we but have men and women mighty in prayer, some victories would be recorded on our side ere long. It is not given to all men to fight; your work then must be done on your knees if not in the battle-field. Either on the hill with the rod in hand, or on the plain with the sword, we must do our best to win the day. One of the bravest of Christian soldiers, scarred with many a fight, said, "I will therefore that men pray everywhere, lifting up holy hands."

How much even the mightiest of men are dependent upon others much weaker than themselves! It was well for the fortunes of the day that Moses was not alone. Moses' hands were heavy. How dependent the soul is compelled to be upon the body. If the flesh is weak, the soul cannot strike a vigorous blow. The soldiers of Israel would watch the rod of Moses; they would soon learn to foretell victory or defeat, as the arms went up or down. Aaron and Hur were wise enough to stay up the wearied muscles, and his hands were steady until the going down of the sun. So we next read, Joshua discomfited Amalek.

Some of my readers are not prominent men, like either Moses or Joshua. But you, too, have your part to play. Do you stay up the hands of Moses, or is your influence bearing them down? "The one on the one side, the other on the other side." It took two of them; they could not be at both sides at once. If you can do nothing else, you may bear up those who lead others in prayer. How the soldiers would bless those who were holding up the arms that seemed like the arms of God! Let us then, if we can do nothing else, see to it that all our influence is to bear up, and not to bear down, those who turn the tide of battle, and win the victories which make angels sing, Hallelujah!

An altar marked the place of battle, and glory was given to the Lord of Hosts. Though the aching limbs of Moses would for many a day tell of his efforts in turning the battle that day, yet he called the altar, "The Lord is my banner." It is a touching sight to see the flags of our own country hanging up in St. Paul's. What a history they have! What bravery has focussed itself round that old rag of silk, and what historic names are embroidered upon it! and yet, when new colours have taken their places, the brave hearts send their honoured old flag to the national temple. And shall not we, who are the soldiers of the cross, call the battle-fields where we have won our bravest fights by the name of Him to whom we ascribe all might and majesty? Nay, when the last fight has been won, and the enemy of our race for ever defeated, we shall unite in singing, "NOT UNTO US, O LORD, NOT UNTO US, BUT UNTO THY NAME GIVE GLORY!

VII.

THE HEAVENLY WORKMAN.

EPHESIANS ii. 10.

THIS chapter contains an argument which is a good illustration of the two-edged way in which the sword of the Spirit cuts enemies who come from different directions. On the one hand, Paul strikes at those who would teach licentiousness possible to men who are saved by grace. We are His workmanship, created in Christ Jesus, unto *good works*. It is true that we do not improve ourselves. It is all of grace, yet good works are binding upon us all the more. On the other hand, let us not take any credit to ourselves. If we are elevated or refined, it is because God has taken pains with us, or we should be as coarse and foul as anyone.

Indeed, we should never have come into the workshop but for the heavenly artist. "No man can come to me, except the Father which hath sent me draw him." It is as old Mr. Honest said, when the rest of the pilgrims came to watch him cross the river. This blunt, staunch old pilgrim said, "Grace reigns."

Without entering further into the argument, it will be worth our while to consider some of the ideas suggested by the figure used, namely, that God works with skill and industry in elevating and refining human nature; and let us not overlook the fact that there is A GREAT DIFFERENCE IN THE MATERIAL.

It is useless to say that all men are equal. We are not all born alike. From the fault or misfortune of our progenitors, we may start on the race with heavy burdens that we cannot shake off. Besides, we differ in both physical and mental constitution. We use terms which are very suggestive when we speak of a "hard" man, or when we say, "He is soft," "He is coarse," or "He is a fine man." Some we describe as Nature's gentlemen, while others are born mean. Let it be understood that the Great Workman does not expect the same results from every kind of material. There is one thing He expects from all, and something He has a right to expect, and that is what all can do: we must love God. That being so, there may be many other things in which we differ from our fellows; but every one who loves God will some day be with God. Let us then be charitable with each other. Why should I be hard on another Christian because he differs from me? Perhaps he has to make a great effort to tolerate me. Let all the material in God's workshop remember that whatever comes there comes to be beautified. While this thought will help me to bear with my fellow-Christian, because I know that he will be improved before he leaves, so it will teach me to be modest, inasmuch as I should not be there if I were perfect!

Is it Ruskin who defines Art as that which "gives form to thought and beauty to utility"? How well this applies to God, the Great Workman. He is the Almighty Artist. Every other artist is limited, if in nothing else, certainly in time; but not so with Him who is at work before us. There is no limit to His powers of invention, or to the time He has at His disposal. He needs no candle! How He shows His art in the grace He gives the humblest material. It is easy to recognise His hand. There is wondrous individuality about His work. The other day, the writer was dining in the new home of an old friend, and saw before him a painting that seemed like Wilson's work, and said to the host, "Is that a Wilson?" It turned out to be so. And God does not need to engrave His name on His work. The fact is, whatever God touches He ennobles. Just as whatever the hand of Michael Angelo wrought bore the mark of his genius, whether in clay or bronze, so with *His* workmanship. Whether it is a coarse, or soft, or hard man He takes in hand, the man must be the better for it. For instance, what different men Elijah and Elisha were,—the one so rugged, the other so tender,—one best fitted to live in the mountain cave, the other feeling most at home in the domestic circle; yet both of them were fashioned by God, and bore the impress of His wonder-working hand. Elijah was the grander man, but Elisha would be the most beloved. Do not be disheartened because you are inferior to someone else. Remember that a penny is as much a coin of the realm as a sovereign.

IT IS WELL FOR US TO HAVE CONFIDENCE IN THE WORKMAN.—What a different fate awaits some of the blocks of marble which come into London as compared with others. They will all be used, but how differently. One is taken to the studio of the sculptor, to be carved into some statue to be admired for ages; another is sawn into slabs to make the counter of some gin palace! If the former block could know and feel the difference, how glad it would be to find itself in the places where statues are made. Let those of us who are lovers of God never forget that we are in the studio. It is not the purpose of the Heavenly Workman to put us to any of the baser uses we might have been fit for but for His grace. "Who hath delivered us from the power of darkness, and hath translated us into the kingdom of His dear Son." God means to make us that which He can contemplate with delight, and we may be sure that every improvement in us brings Him enjoyment. "He taketh pleasure in the work of His hands."

This ought to reconcile us to what sometimes seems hard treatment. We must learn to trust the Workman at such times. A statue is not finished without some violence. The great mallet and chisel are used, knocking off large pieces, and to anyone who did not know, it would seem as though the square block of marble was about to be destroyed. But not so; the sculptor sees the thing of beauty in the rude block. And in like manner God can see in us, even when unregenerate, what He designs us for. Is there some one reading this who is passing through great sorrow on account of sin? It seems as though you can never be happy again. Ah, you are in the rough stage; but God has not done with you. When He has finished, He will leave a smile on the face that shall never change to sorrow. Confidence in the Workman will give us patience when He seems long. We are ready to sing—

> "Finish, then, Thy new creation,
> Pure and spotless let us be."

Yes, all in good time. He has His own reasons for being slow. He is never in a hurry. He can sleep when His disciples are in great fear. But we are safe while He sleeps, and He does not need to make haste.

WE MUST NOT FORGET THAT THE WORKMAN HAS A PLAN.—Life in any of us is a very complicated affair. Things are always happening—births, deaths, and marriages. Business relations alter. Circumstances differ: there seems no order or arrangements. It is chaos to us. And yet God knows all, and knows the precise bearing of each event on our lives. It does not seem like it, and yet, if we look back, we may often see that God has been working all along in harmony with one idea. Some time ago, when in Manchester, the writer saw the men at work pulling down whole streets of houses to make room for a new railway station. All appeared ruin and disorder. Here was a party digging out foundations; in another place the bricklayers were building walls; elsewhere some one was setting out for other walls; beyond them they were still pulling down. It seemed like chaos, and yet in the architect's office could be seen the elevation and picture of the complete whole. Every man was working to a plan. And so God has His elevation, but He does not show it. "It doth not yet appear." When Joseph was in jail, he was in the path of Providence, and the fetters of iron were as much part of the plan as the chain of gold he wore when brought to the summit of greatness.

What a variety of tools!—What are the so-called means of grace but tools in the hand of the Great Workman? What are preachers but God's chisels and hammers? "Is not Thy word a hammer?" And therefore we should be thankful for them, and when we come to the place where the Word is preached, we should expect to go out better than we came in. Nor should we be impatient if there is a preacher who does not suit us. It may not be our turn, for while you are saying, "I cannot get any good under him," some one else says, "Bless that man, he always does me good!" Not but what some of us would be the better for sharpening. When I see the mason's lad taking some scores of chisels to the forge to be sharpened, I wish he could take as many ministers to undergo the same process. For no preacher ought to be dull!

Books too are tools. How much the Great Workman has accomplished by the press! Without naming the Bible, how many times we have known a good book to produce some feature of refinement in us. Some of us have never been the same since we read some religious books. How important is the work of those who write them! Especially sacred poetry has, in the hands of the blessed Spirit, been used to strengthen faith and confirm hope. Dr. Watts spoke the experience of thousands of the saints of God when he said,—

> "Thus, Lord, while we remember Thee,
>   We blest and pious grow;
> By hymns of praise we learn to be
>   Triumphant here below."

But the finest work is often done by those sharp-edged chisels called Pain and Bereavement. How many of us are to be made perfect by suffering! It is not the dull tool that can cut the fine lines. There are some of us who owe whatever is beautiful in us to the days when our joys were stunned and left for dead. Even the Christ—let it be said reverently—would not be all to us He is and must ever be, if no tear had ever run down His cheek, and if His laughter was louder than His sobs! He will always be the dearer to us for having had to cry, "My God, why hast Thou forsaken me?"

Will the work ever be completed? Not in this world certainly. There is no room for self-complacence. God has even in this world made some glorious beings out of flesh and blood. Moses, Elijah, Paul, are His workmanship, and yet none of these ever thought that he had climbed where there were no loftier heights. One thing is apparent,—we shall begin in heaven where we leave off in this world, just as the student begins at the University where he leaves off at school.

Where are you going? In the quarry you may see the blocks of marble waiting to be put on the trucks; but before they are sent off they are marked with the initials of their destined owner. You are allowed to choose your eternal position. Jesus stands beside you ready to mark you with His cross. Shall He do it?

VIII.

THE LADDER.

GENESIS xxviii. 12.

WHO can tell what his children may come to? We know not their future. After all our love and care, they may be tramps in a casual ward! Who would have predicted that such a mother's lad as Jacob was would have to sleep with a stone for his pillow? But what a number of mothers' pets are private soldiers, or before the mast! Or, worse still, with feet soddened with rain, walking the streets! Rebekah had herself to thank for much of her grief. She taught Jacob to cheat his father and brother. Esau said, "When father is dead,

I will cut Jacob's throat;" and he was very likely to keep his word, so the darling of his mother must tramp for it. Isaac lived to see the wanderer return a rich man, but Rebekah "died without the sight." Even in the best-trained families there may be stray sheep; but it is possible to covenant with God, so that the wanderer may, all unknown to himself, be bound to the throne of Omnipotence.

While Jacob slept, "behold a ladder." He had not thought of God when he lay down, but here was a way up from earth to heaven, and God at the top. Is it stretching a figure too much to say that it is a picture of Jesus? Had not the Lord Himself this ladder in His mind when He said to the first disciples, "Hereafter ye shall see heaven open, and the angels of God ascending and descending upon the Son of Man"?

> " Jesus that ladder is,
>   The incarnate Deity,

> Partaker of celestial bliss,
>   And human misery;
> Sent from His high abode
>   To sleeping mortals given,
> He stands, and man unites to God,
> And earth connects with heaven."

JESUS, THE LADDER, CONNECTS EARTH TO HEAVEN.—There is a way from this sinful world to the pure heaven. Jesus is the connecting link. Adam was; but sin broke the chain, and the world would have been adrift but for Jesus. Christ is the new and living way. No amount of sin in the world can break the communication. He is "the way of holiness." There is no part of the world this ladder does not touch. Think of the number of climbers. Who shall count the children of all countries who pass by Christ to heaven? All countries are represented on the ladder. Then the angels, bright and fair, passing on errands of mercy to the elect, sent forth to minister for them who shall be heirs of salvation,—are they not helping the saints up the ladder? As we look towards the top, we see some who are nearing the end of the journey. Already the glory is shining on their features. Others are just stepping into heaven. What a change for them! And their feeling is ever;—We could not have been here but for the ladder. Do these who have gained the top regret what they left behind? Do they ever wish that they had held on to the world? Oh, how small the world looks from the top, and the gold or the pleasures are but shadows now.

Are all my readers on this ladder? There is no other that can take you right. If you are not believing in Jesus, you are on the highway to ruin. You may not walk in the dirt, but you are in the way to hell if out of Christ. Why should you not start for glory to-day? Begin to climb, if you have not done so. Take hold of Jesus, and you will find taking hold will lift you up the first few steps. "Must I not give this up, and that up?" Yes, you must, but in trusting your soul to the atonement, you will find yourself lifted well out of the mire!

THIS LADDER COMES TO SINNERS.—They have not to fetch it. "Say not in thine heart, Who shall ascend into heaven, that is, to bring Christ?—The word is nigh thee." God does not wait till we ask before He sends salvation. He offers it to us. The supplanter was surprised; he had not expected this sign of the favour of God. It was wonderful that it should come to him, when he had not put up a prayer. What is the proclamation of the Gospel but the coming of the ladder-foot to the sleeping sinner? We should not have been astonished, had Jacob made a sacrifice before he slept, to have seen the ladder in the smoke of the offering: but to come unasked, —ah, that is how it is! If God had to wait for us to begin, He would never have one sinner saved. "*I am Alpha.*" Just as you cannot spell the word salvation without the letter a, so you cannot have heaven without Jesus. He begins the work. None of us can say, We have not been asked to climb. God calls, Jesus beckons, angels whisper, saints, ascending, shout, Come! You cannot be in the wrong place to start for heaven. There was a path from the swine troughs to the Father's house. The vilest of men may start, if he will but take hold of Jesus. One of the most foul-mouthed of men became a preacher for Jesus, and wrote a hymn that has been sung by millions of climbers :—

> "The God of Abraham praise,
> At whose supreme command
> From earth I rise and seek the joys
> At His right hand."

GOD IS AT THE TOP, SPEAKING KIND WORDS DOWN THE LADDER.—Jacob saw the Lord above, and heard Him say, "I am the Lord God of Abraham thy father."

"Behold, I am with thee," "I will not leave thee." Think of this—God speaking kind words to the supplanter! Yes, and it is so now. Christ is God's own plan. The ladder whose foot is on the earth came down from heaven. Can the Divine Being be anything else but delighted with Jesus? So much so that sometimes when Jesus was here below, a voice was heard saying, "This is my beloved Son." Do you see yonder life-boat coming back through the surf?—she is filled with men and women taken off the wreck. Among the people on the shore, the most excited and pleased at the sight is the gentleman who gave the boat to that place. No wonder that he shouts words of encouragement, as the poor creatures tremble at the sight of the rollers breaking on the coast.

Let such of my readers as are on the ladder, encourage others to start. Shout aloud for joy. If we only believed what

God has said about His heaven, we should look happy, and our faces would invite others to come the same way. The smiles of God's elect would encourage others to venture. Should, however, the coldness of the Church have daunted any one from making a start, let him be persuaded to look higher up. See the Lord in all His majesty, delighting in what? Mercy! Yes, listen for yourself. Do not let any one pretend to interpret for you: God speaks in the plainest of words—"*Come unto me.*"

Suffer a few words of ADVICE TO CLIMBERS.—To those who read this book that mean to reach the top, we would say, *Be sure to get the right ladder;* there are plenty of shams. We need not say anything about Popery. That does not pretend to take men to the top: the end of their ladder is purgatory. When masses are said for the repose of dead Cardinals and Popes, other poor sinners must not think of heaven.

Formalism is a sham ladder. It is rotten, and is sure to let men down. Besides, it is too short. Hear the man who is going up: "I fast twice in the week, I give tithes, I am not as other men." He is at the top; he cannot get any farther. How different to the man who is climbing up by Jesus! We can hear him sing. They are wondrous sweet, these ladder songs. Listen!

> "I see stretched out to save me
> The arm of my Redeemer;
> That arm shall quell
> The powers of hell,
> And silence the blasphemer.
>
> I render Thee the glory,
> I know Thou wilt deliver,
> But let me rise
> Above the skies,
> And praise Thy love for ever.

Morality is of no use as a ladder. It got broken in the fall, and all the bottom rounds are out. You see all ten of them are gone. You cannot reach the bottom step!

Take firm hold.—You will want both hands. If you could see those who have fallen, you might learn what was the cause. See, one had a money-bag; as it got heavier he had to take both hands to it, and down he came. Another has a theatre ticket; another, a woman, has a letter,—it is an offer of marriage. Jesus is not to be trifled with. Grasp Him as a drowning man does a rope, and even of good works say,—

> " Nothing in my hands I bring,
> Simply to Thy cross I cling."

Don't look down, or you will be giddy.—Looking down on others will make you feel how well you have done to climb so far, and keep on so long. If Peter had not looked down, he might have kept from a bad fall. It is true he got up and started again, but, as you know, he went with a bad limp for many a long day. This is true not only of young Christians, but men fifty years of age are in much more slippery places than they think for. Look up: one look at God will steady you.

As an old Yorkshireman once said, *Don't come down to fetch any one else up.*—Is not that the reason why some are much lower down than they were years ago? Ask that young woman the cause of her trouble, and it is, "He promised he would go with me, and now, not only does he refuse to do so, but he tries to prevent me!" If your friends will not follow you up, leave them behind, and join with those on the ladder who sing:

> " My old companions, fare you well,
>   I cannot go with you to hell ;
>   I mean with Jesus Christ to dwell,
>   Let me go ! "

X.

FINDING THE TRIBUTE-MONEY.

MATTHEW xvii. 27.

THE Gospels tell us, not only of the greater actions of Jesus, but of some things that are so small that few people care to meditate upon them; and yet, some of these smaller deeds are very beautiful. Glorious as was the miracle of the raising of Lazarus, the most beautiful thing in the incident is the tears on Christ's cheek. He raised others from the dead, but it was left for John to tell of his Master's sympathy, in the words never to be forgotten, "Jesus wept." The story we are now writing about is not one of the great miracles, and yet its lessons are well worth our careful study.

There is what, for the want of a better word, we must call THE MODESTY OF JESUS. Rather than offend the prejudices of the people, He would waive His claim. The men whose business it was to collect the Temple dues, asked Peter if his Master did not pay tribute? Yes, said the man of ready speech, and that without consulting the Master. When he reached the house where Jesus was, he was anticipated by Christ asking him, "Of whom do the kings of the earth take tribute? of their own children, or strangers?" Of strangers, replied Peter. "Then are the children free." That is, I, being the Son of God, surely need not to pay towards the repairs of my Father's house. But rather than those who do not acknowledge my Divine Sonship should think I am careless about the Temple, I will pay. He would rather pay than be a stumbling-block.

Are not we, who call ourselves His disciples,

too ready to put forth our titles to men's respect, and to stand upon our dignity? We might learn from our Lord, who never arrayed Himself in the style He might have done. He put on the menial's livery, "made Himself of no reputation." As soon as we gain a stripe, we are so eager to have it sewn on our uniform. We do not like to miss a single parade without our comrades knowing they must touch their caps to us. The Apostle Paul had to complain in his day, "All seek their own, not Jesus Christ's." He was a notable example of the contrary. For though he was chief apostle, when at Corinth he worked for his bread, and preferred to sit at the loom for many weary hours, rather than irritate those narrow-minded Christians who did not like paying their ministers. At Philippi he was tied up and flogged, when he could have stopped the proceedings by simply telling them that he was a Roman. Might there not be more peace in the Church if we were more like our Master—not too anxious to push our claims, and to come to the front? And in family life, how many breaches might be prevented if we were willing to forego our claims, and give way to others; it is this being "righteous over much" in our demands, it is claiming the uttermost farthing, which causes so much irritation. How many lawsuits might be prevented if there were a little more of the "nevertheless." Let us not be too exacting, but seek the spirit of Christ, "Who, for the joy set before Him, *endured the cross.*"

We learn something of THE POVERTY OF JESUS. Yes, if ever there was a poor man, it was the Lord of life and glory. He did not take fees when He healed the sick, or He would not have been so familiar with want. He had not fifteen pence, when He needed it for church dues. Do not let us worry because we are obliged to sit on the free seats. Christ could not have afforded to pay pew rent. Let us not chafe ourselves with the thought of our poverty. There is no disgrace in being short of money. We need not be ignoble because we are poor. We may win honour if we have an empty pocket, and the Victoria cross looks well on a private's jacket!

There is something of greater moment than wealth, and that is character. Money may not elevate, good deeds do. You may put a diamond ring in a swine's snout, and it will not cease to grunt. Let us not look at our banking account to see how much we are worth. We touch our hats to a man because, as we say, he is worth half a million of money, when the real truth is, he is not worth the clothes he stands in. It is true, the bank would honour any cheque he draws, but in heaven they have no mansion waiting for him. In the conventional meaning of the words, Christ was not worth fifteen pence; yet He could heal the sick and raise the dead. It will be worth our while to weigh ourselves in the true balances, and to find out Heaven's assessment of our belongings.

On the other hand, this story gives us A PEEP INTO CHRIST'S RESOURCES. Though He had not the money by Him, He knew where it was. The gold and silver are all His. He it was who laid the golden streaks in the river beds of California. He knew of this money in the fish's mouth. How did it get there? Those of us who use the rod and line know a fish will swallow anything bright. Perhaps the coin had fallen out of some child's hand, crossing the ferry, or it may have been in the girdle of some drowned fisherman. What an amount of treasure there must be in the sea! more under the blue waves than in all the banks in the world. It could be brought out if the Lord willed it, and yet His treasury is often empty. Some of us think what good we would do if we had but the gold. This is by no means certain. Depend upon it, with all the work that needs doing, and that cannot begin for the want of money, if God dare but trust His people with riches, He would put us in the way of getting the wealth that now lies waste.

This is true of everything that God needs. He can help Himself to what He wants out of Satan's lockers. Was not Saul of Tarsus as much out of the Church's reach as the piece of money many fathoms deep? And yet Christ put a hook in Satan's nostril, and brought Saul to make many rich by circulating among the heathen. It may be that some of us may live to see the work of God carried on by hands now used to build forts for Satan to occupy. Was not Luther the monk as much hidden as the piece of money? And it may be that from the Romish communion we may get someone who shall be as effective as he was; or that from the companionship of Bradlaugh we may have some notable defender of Christianity.

We do well to learn, however, that GOD DOES NOT OFTEN ACT WITHOUT HUMAN AGENCY. Christ could have done without Peter. It would have been easy to have willed it, and the fish would have swum to His feet as He stood by the side of the lake, and have dropped the coin within his reach. But He knew that Peter could catch the fish, and so he was sent to do what he was able. It appears to be the Divine plan to do what men cannot, but not to act for us. The farmer cannot make the seed germinate; he cannot make the rain to fall, or cause the sun to shine; but he can plough and sow, neither of which God ever does. The mariner cannot make the wind to blow, but he can weigh the anchor, and trim the sails. Creation and industry are partners.

Is it not so in spiritual things? We cannot save ourselves. We cannot atone for sin, but we can believe in the atonement made by Jesus. Without grace we perish, but we can accept the grace which bringeth salvation. This will holds good in Church work. The preacher cannot save a soul by the most powerful appeal, but he can prepare that which interests the congregation. An indolent preacher is a useless one. So in the training of our children: we must work if God is to work with us.

Does not God use the best means within His reach? Peter was a fisherman. It would have been useless to send some other of the apostles. Levi might have stood there till now before he caught a fish. He could prepare a Church schedule, but fishing was not his business. Let us send Peter to the work he is best fitted for. "The round peg too often gets into the square hole."

This story teaches us that HE WHO WORKS FOR JESUS IS SURE TO GET HIS PAY. "That take, and give unto them for thee and me." Christ wanted fifteen pence, and Peter took out of the fish's mouth half-a-crown! And thus, in obeying Christ, he paid his own taxes. In keeping His commandments there is great reward. Let us not stumble at the mystery. Peter might have said, Lord, I never did yet take a fish with money in its mouth: or, Lord, how is the fish to know that it is to come to my hook? The lake has thousands of fish, and yet you say, "The first that cometh up." It was enough for Peter that Christ gave the order. He had learned that commandments are promises, and that for God to say a thing must be done, made it possible.

> "Faith, mighty faith, the promise sees,
>   And looks to that alone;
> Laughs at impossibilities,
>   And cries it shall be done."

If we win anything for Jesus, He will share it with us. "Me and thee." "He that overcometh shall sit down on my throne." "He that reapeth receiveth wages." Are we then among the disciples of Jesus? Is it "Me and thee?" Are you a co-worker with God? If not, there must be personal surrender. We may be in arms against God, but if we submit He is ready to forgive. He will put us in the ranks of His army, and we may yet win spoilt for Christ and ourselves. "Me and thee." Christ will share all He has with His bride. He will endow her with endless beauty and glory. All He has shall be ours. "Me and thee" is the fortune of the believer.

XI.

WAITING IN MERCY'S HOUSE.

JOHN v. 1—14.

WHO wonders that a place which had such a history as that described in this chapter should be called mercy's house? So many people had at different times there obtained mercy, that there is nothing remarkable in the title the place had won. It is worth while to bear in mind that it was close by the *sheep-market.* We should not have been surprised if we had heard of it as being near unto the Temple; but, as if God would teach us that His mercy is to be got wherever sought, the house of mercy is close by the place where money is made; and so, it is not only where the melodious organ fills the fretted aisles with sacred sounds that the sorrowing and helpless soul may meet with mercy, but in the haunts of busy commerce, or anywhere else, the heart that needs consolation may meet with Jesus.

How came the five porches to be built? Had some of those which had found health in the spring built these alcoves for the comfort of seekers for mercy, and thus shown their appreciation of what they had received? It would have been a fitting thing, and it is so yet. Let those who find grace to help in the means provided, see to it that, so far as they have the power, others have the chance of getting the same privileges.

Let us linger at this pool-side, and learn the lessons the Author of this sacred life of Christ intended us to learn. And as we learn, let us write on the walls of these porches, that others coming after us may be all the wiser for our stopping here. In the first porch write up—

IT IS NEVER TOO LATE TO MEND.—It is evident the man whom Jesus saw at the pool-side thought so. One cannot but admit the tenacity with which he clung to the hope of recovery. It was what the late Jabez Bunting liked to call "obstinate faith." Thirty-eight years a victim to the disease, and yet hoping for a cure. How often he had been disappointed! Just as the water was troubled, he made the effort, but had always been too late. Having no one to assist him, he could not drag himself to the pool before someone else who had helpers was in, and healed. One can see him as he smiles a sickly smile, and whispers, "Better luck next time," and goes back to wait the next moving of the waters.

It is more than possible that some of my readers need to be encouraged to hope that it is not too late to be cured of the malady which threatens to destroy the soul. You may be in a sad case, but yet do not despair.

The enemy whispers that it is too late. He holds you by the chains of some sinful habit; but Christ can deliver you, impotent as you are. Perhaps you are held down by some sinful friendship, and may feel that it is quite impossible for you to get free; but God can save, by so changing your life that your companions shall no longer desire your society. Or you may be old, grown grey in vice, yet it is not too late to make those grey hairs a crown of glory, instead of the fool's cap they now are.

Whatever you do, don't lose hope of those of your friends who seem almost too far gone to be recovered. Satan could not wish for anything better than that your hopes should die, and your prayers cease. There are men hanging over the pit of destruction to-day; the rope that holds them is parting: see, some of the strands are worn through. Education, godly training, respect for the sabbath, reverence for the name of God,—all these are gone: only a mother's prayers hold them from the flame. Pray on, let not despair cut the last thread that holds them this side the pit. Read what we have written in the first of the porches:—

It is never too late to mend.

And now let us visit the second porch, and write up another of the lessons we learn at the pool-side. WAITING ON THE LORD IS TRUE WISDOM.—If you don't wish to grow worse, keep in mercy's house. Do not be persuaded to give up going to the place of worship you have attended, though you know that 'tis but outward show. How pleased the enemy of your soul would be if he could but persuade you to spend the whole of your life away from God. As it is, there is at least an hour each week in which you are among those who praise and pray. You have heard the master whom you have served faithfully in all but this whisper, What is the use of going to a place of worship when your heart is so hard? What is the use of ever looking into the Bible, or listening to sermons? Do not these things make you uncomfortable? Why do you continue in them? Ah, my friend, don't listen to him! It is the one thing which keeps hope alive. "Faith cometh by hearing." Do not close the last avenue of hope.

It may be that some of my readers have been long convinced of sin, and yet never able to rejoice in God our Saviour. You are tempted to give up. "Why go where sin is denounced and Christ preached? You are no happier. Better attend some more fashionable place, where the preacher deals in generalities, and does not give such home thrusts." So people might have said to this man, "Why keep going to the pool? What better are you? You are only made to feel greater disappointment. Someone will get in before you again, and you will be left as bad as ever." Supposing such counsels had prevailed, and the poor man had stayed at home the day Christ visited the place? There is no wisdom like waiting. He was a wise man who said, "If I die without salvation, I will die at the feet of the Saviour." Wait on the Lord, I say, and while waiting, sing,—

> "Jesus, take my sins away,
> And make me know Thy name;
> Thou art now as yesterday,
> And evermore the same.
>
> Thou my true Bethesda be:
> I know within Thine arms is room;
> All the world may unto Thee,
> Their house of mercy, come."

Let us visit the third porch, and write up, in bright, cheerful tints, another of the sweet lessons learned here. CHRIST IS THE SHORT WAY TO COMFORT. The pool was called the house of mercy, but Christ was mercy itself. All mere human instrumentalities are to Jesus what the house is to the Master. We have in this story an indication of Christ's plan of saving men. The poor man did not ask Jesus to heal him. It was mercy who took the initiative, and said, Wilt thou be made whole? Do any of my readers wish to be cured of sin? If so, He asks, Do you wish for salvation? not, mind you, Do you wish to escape hell? That may be the beginning of repentance; the fear of hell has led some to seek the Lord, but it is not the only wish in the penitent heart. There are many who love sin as much as ever, yet would like to escape hell. If such were to die, and as the soul left the body, had to pass the gates, and was told to choose which gate you will enter—one is the door of hell and the other the gate of heaven—of course the gate of bliss would be chosen; but that is not what Jesus asks us. It is, Will you be made holy? Will you become like me? Is not this the true reason of so many remaining unsaved? They do not wish to be good; they hate the restriction of virtue; they don't wish to have to deny self. They say, Give us heaven, because we fear hell, but don't let heaven begin below!

Mark that Christ gave a command as well as asked a question. "*Take up thy bed and walk.*" This was something that was a physical impossibility; yet the man made the effort, and was helped of God, and so was made whole. What does Jesus say to you? Mind, not to everybody, but to those who are willing to be saved,—not to those who want heaven rather than holiness, but to those who wish to be like Jesus? He says, "Believe on me." Why say you cannot believe? God's commandments are promises. He never commands what He will not help us to do. "Believe that I am your surety, that I have answered for your guilt, not hoping that you might fulfil the law's demands; but knowing that you would not, I have suffered for you; I promised to pay your debt, and I have paid it." Show that you believe this by rejoicing in Jesus. You cannot believe without peace coming to your heart. Can I illustrate this? Suppose that you are a young tradesman, and that by some bad debts you have made, your money is gone, and you have had to overdraw your account at the bank. You receive a note from the manager, asking you to call; you do so, when he tells you that he cannot let you go on, and that if you don't settle before to-morrow he will sell you up! You are in despair, but in the afternoon another note from the manager; you know the handwriting, and fear to break the seal, just as you feel about reading your Bible. At last you do so, and read that an old friend has heard of your difficulties, and told the bank that he will be your surety, and as he is rich, his name stands good for you. Now, if you believe this, can you do anything but rejoice? Who would laugh at you if you were to leap for joy? Just so, and if you will read the 53rd of Isaiah, you will see that "the Lord hath laid on Him the iniquities of us all." Believe that, and you cannot but be happy.

In the next of the porches we will write up another of the lessons we learn here, namely, THE NEWLY SAVED MAY EXPECT A CHECK.

The man who had been impotent, but had been healed, was met as he was going down the street by those who objected to his carrying his bed. One would have thought that their delight in seeing him cured would have overcome their regard for the letter of the law. But it has ever been so; no sooner do we obtain a blessing from God than some one or other objects to our joy in it. Should some one read this who has recently been much blessed of God, do not be surprised if some one tries to rob you of your new-found joy. And most likely it will be some one who ought to have been the last to do so. There are not a few, even of those who are amongst the friends of God, who don't see the full meaning of "Rejoice with them that do rejoice." They cannot understand the enthusiasm of those who have experienced a great deliverance. They themselves had never been in the far country, and cannot tell why there should be such rejoicings over the return of him who "spent all and began to be in want." Do not let us be found amongst those who would stop the man who now carries that which once carried him!

And to those of my readers who have just been made happy in Jesus, let me say, Let not anyone stop you from joy in the Lord, it is your strength. But do not be surprised if you meet with those who wish to stop you. See, here they come; listen to them for a moment. "What, you rejoicing in God? Take care that you are not presuming! Do you think that you have repented as you ought to have done? Would it not be more seemly if one so wicked as you have been had wept more bitterly, and waited longer at the gate of repentance?" Say, He who made me whole, said, Carry thy bed. Here is another of these would-be critics of Jesus. "What, rejoicing? Don't you know that we live in a wicked world, and that you may soon fall?" Yes. I know all that, but He who forgave me has promised me strength to hold on to the end. And He would take me to heaven, to save me from hell.

Have we not here the secret of much of the religious persecutions which have disgraced Christianity? The newly-liberated soul, fresh from the presence of the Saviour, daring to rejoice without the permission of the Church. What are the victories of

Protestantism but the carrying of the bed, in spite of the Sanhedrim? Let us listen to Jesus. If He says, Take up thy bed and walk, do as He bids you, in spite of priest or presbytery.

There is yet one porch we have not entered. There, too, we will write up a sentence, in bold black capitals. It is this— SIN WILL HURT YOU MORE THAN DISEASE. Jesus found the man in the temple; He could not have found him in a better place. The last words spoken by our Lord are very significant: "*Sin no more, lest a worse thing come unto thee.*" What, worse than eight-and-thirty years of such torment as I have had? Yes! What is that something worse? It is not for me to dwell upon it now, only to say that preachers nowadays seem afraid to use the language Jesus used concerning the punishment of sin. Surely He knew what He was about. Let us not try to persuade ourselves that we are more tender than He was. He whose kind heart would not allow him to look on that impotent man without giving him relief, told him that if he sinned again he might suffer still more than he had done. Was he less kind in the temple than at the pool-side?

Beware, then, of sin! It leads to more than physical pain. There are those in hell who would gladly change places with those who are now on beds of agony. We know they were wise of whom it is said, "*Others were tortured not accepting deliverance.*" They preferred the stake to hell fire, and the gloom of the dungeon to the darkness of the prison-house where God's felons are confined.

XII.

A GOOD MAN'S BAD SON.

"*And departed without being desired.*"—2 CHRON. xxi. 20.

FOLLY is often the father of sin. It was so in the history we are about to study. Jehoshaphat was a very good man; no one can read his biography and not admire him; and yet he had a weakness which well-nigh proved fatal to himself, and certainly was ruin to his household, though there was a great deal of that which is lovely about the king of Judah. He was pious and gentle, devoted to the welfare of his people, taking great pains to lead them in the path of virtue; but there was one glaring inconsistency which undid a great deal of the good he would otherwise have effected.

And here let us note a lesson for parents, which is this—FOLLY IN FATHERS MAY BECOME SIN IN THEIR SONS. The pious king showed his children a good example, so far as we know, in everything but his love for the society of the ungodly and worldly. He was friendly with Ahab. This friendship nearly cost him his life at the battle of Ramoth-Gilead, and lost him wealth by the wreck of the navy he had built to go with the ships of Ahaziah, king of Israel. The children of Jehoshaphat did not leave off where their father did. We may feel ourselves strong enough to go nearer to sin than some good people dare to do. We run a fearful risk in this way, and often forget that we cannot go alone, whether we do well or ill. Our children are sure to imitate us, and they may not have the same love for the right that we have, and so, like as Jehoram was not content to be merely on visiting terms with Ahab, but married his daughter, if we are not careful, we may take our children where they may choose to stop, instead of going back with us.

Perhaps this is more true of folly than sin. It often happens that bad men have good children. Shocked by the crimes of their father, the sons will recoil from the sin which brings misery to their home. On the other hand, seeing that the conduct of their father does not produce much outward mischief, they rush on to their ruin, and the old man's grey hairs are brought down with sorrow to the grave, and the tears scald the withered cheek all the more because conscience whispers, "You showed the lads the way." For instance. Let a man be fond of his glass. Not a drunkard, "but likes a drop of something good," and yet does not neglect his business, or is ever seen to be what is called "the worse for liquor," yet the decanters are always about, and anything is an excuse for "something hot." In such a case, it does not need a prophet to see that some one or more of the lads will kill himself with drink one of these days. He will not have the power to stop himself, or will, by the time he has got to like the glass, have made himself companions of a very different kind to those his father has, —men who rather like to be "merry," and who have no objection to going home now and then decidedly drunk. We know what this leads to. If we are not careful in this matter of strong drink, we may have to mourn over the grave of our sons killed before their prime, and laid in a drunkard's grave.

Or let a father be unwise in his treatment of the Sabbath Day. Let him not be a Sabbath breaker in the ordinary sense of the word,—never going a-pleasuring on the Lord's Day, but not hesitating, if there is a popular preacher to be heard, to leave his place at the head of his own pew, to run after some novelty. It was too far to walk, and so he must ride,—there was no help for it. What is there to wonder at if, when the boys are men, they never, or but rarely, sit where their old father does on the Lord's Day? Very likely, when little boys, they rode in the "underground" or some tram on the Sunday, and they don't see that there is more sin in riding a mile or two farther, though it was not to a preaching, but pleasuring. It is not too much to say that very often we see that sermon hunters breed Sabbath breakers.

Take another case. Here is a father who is not a liar; you would wrong him, it may be, if you described him as such; and yet he can sail very near the wind. He would not tell a bare-faced lie, but he does not mind very much if a customer deceives himself. "Why should I tell him? he ought to know his business." What must this do for children and servants? Is there anything to be wondered at if they allow him to deceive himself, and then go on from that to actual dishonesty and deceit. Let parents show their children how safely they can walk on the edge of the precipice, and some day they will see the child they love the most fall over. Jehoram *walked in the way of the kings of Israel, like as did the house of Ahab*, but it was his father, good king Jehoshaphat, that taught him the way to the dwelling of Ahab!

This brings us to another lesson, taught by the history of this bad man, which is—OUR WEDDING DAY MAY BE THE WORST DAY'S WORK WE EVER DID. It was so with Jehoram. "*He had the daughter of Ahab to wife.*" He had been used to go to the palace of the king of Israel, and soon was infatuated with the beauty of Jezebel's daughter. Most young folks look forward to marrying, and having a home of their own,—and very properly so, too; but too often there is not enough consideration about the kind of man or woman we are going to marry. It is not enough that he is rich, or that she is beautiful: what is money, or good looks even? One is round and rolls away, and the other is but skin deep. It is well to ask, "What sort of a family does he belong to?" "I like to marry into a good stock," said one. Yes, and if we were as particular about men and women as we are about our flocks and herds, we should save money and tears. There is many a man who is very careful as to the breeding of his cattle and sheep, and yet will never enquire or care about the pedigree of the girl his son is to marry. She has a lot of money, and yet, if he thought of it, he could not help but see that either a fool or a knave might be grandson to him, and no wonder either.

Don't marry into Ahab's family, whatever there may be of wealth or beauty. Let

Ahab have Jezebel, and let them breed their own kind: why should we have them mixed with us? It is not for nothing that Holy Writ tells us, "*The sons of God saw the daughters of men that they were fair,*" and directly afterwards we read, "*And God saw that the wickedness of man was great in the earth.*" These things go together now, and we cannot marry the houses of Jehoshaphat and Ahab together without bringing new sorrows into the world. "*For he had the daughter of Ahab to wife, and he wrought that which was evil in the eyes of the Lord.*" Sometimes, when we see a man or woman marrying into the house of Ahab, we can foresee the evil, and, in spite of bright skies, orange blossom, and the noise of laughter, we could weep in silence, for we can see the shadow of evil, and hear the steps of coming doom! It is all in vain that the bells ring merry peals. To us we feel that it is a mockery, and we are ready to say,

"Toll, oh, toll, ye bells! Toll for dead hope! Toll for laughter soon to die! Toll for past joys never more to return! Toll, toll, ye bells, for despair will be the fruit of this transient joy! Wedding days are the prelude to the funeral of happiness when the house of Jehoshaphat marries into the doomed house of Ahab!"

What followed this wedding? The pious king was carried to his fathers, and "Jehoram his son reigned in his stead." The three score years and ten were soon over, but before the father died, he took pains, as he thought, to leave his property so that all his sons should be in comfort. He had considerable property, and he left each son both gold, and silver, and fenced cities, but to the firstborn he gave the kingdom. But no sooner had the wicked king got strong in his new position than he used his power to make himself still richer: he greedily grasped at the possession of his brothers.

A GOOD MAN'S BAD SON.

From what we know of the bloodthirsty character of Athaliah, it is more than probable that this was the prompting of the daughter of Jezebel. To get the wealth of his brothers he must take their lives, and so very soon he was the only one of Jehoshaphat's sons left! All the others had been assassinated.

And here we are taught another lesson —HE WHO REBELS AGAINST GOD MUST EXPECT HIS INFERIORS TO REBEL AGAINST HIM. At the first Jehoram had it all his own way; he slew his brethren and took their wealth, but very soon trouble came from another quarter. Edom rebelled against Judah. They refused to pay tribute, and although Jehoram made war, it was all in vain, for though at the first he won a victory, yet the result of the campaign was against Judah. Libnah next revolted. Worse and worse; the warlike Philistines and Arabians combined against the king of Judah, and, coming to his royal city, pillaged it, and carried away his wives and children, so that only one of his sons was left to him. If we rebel against God, we must not be surprised if we have to struggle against rebellion in those beneath us. If we rob God, why should we be astonished if banks break, or those we trust commit fraud? We are only reaping what we have sown. If we disobey our Father which is in heaven, shall we complain if our children are unnatural? God is not the only one who has to say, "*I have nourished and brought up children, and they have rebelled against me.*" Let us resolutely continue to disobey God, following our own desires, and refusing to listen to His commands, or to heed His rebuke, and then we shall fit ourselves to be trampled under foot of those who used to tremble at our voice, and we may have to say of those beneath us what the King of heaven has said of us: "*I have stretched out my hand and no man regarded."* Jehoram died in the bloom of manhood, but he lived long enough to see that *"he that soweth iniquity shall reap vanity."*

There is yet another bitter moral in this tragic tale—THE WORD OF GOD MAY BECOME OUR WORST ENEMY.

Elijah had no good thing for the house of Ahab. There was no love lost between them. He was able to foresee the evil that would come through the unholy alliance. He saw that robbery and murder would be the fruit of the marriage, and he wrote a letter to the king, which seems to have been given to him after the translation of the prophet. In this writing is foretold the doom of the bloody king; he was told that because he had slain better men than himself he should die a painful and loathsome death. And so it came to pass. How Jehoram must have trembled when first the internal pain foretold his doom! It was useless for physicians to prescribe,—there was no remedy for the plague of God. He who had so consistently rebelled against right, and God, found that his own body had rebelled against him. No longer would nerves and muscles obey his will; and he died amidst tortures of the most dreadful character. And all along the writing which came from the man of God would stare him in the face. What was the use of doctors writing a prescription? there was one already written, which could not fail, and so he must die.

What shall we do in the face of this sad story? Shall we not listen to the voice of God, as it calls us to repentance and faith in His Son? Shall we not accept the offer of Divine mercy and forgiveness, and sue for pardon ere it be too late? None of us need go where Jehoram has gone. God is never more in earnest than when He offers pardon to those that will forsake their sins, and trust in His Son; but if we keep on refusing we may find in old age or premature fatal sickness that the very promises scourge us more keenly than the warnings of Scripture. The sermon we have heard and despised, may knot the lash which conscience uses to whip the heart.

Jehoram was but forty years of age when he was carried to his unwept and dishonoured tomb. Let not those of us who are the children of the godly forget that this hated and miserable man was the firstborn of Jehoshaphat. His people made no burning for him, like the burning of his fathers, and, though he was buried in the city of David, it was not in the royal tomb. His history in the Book of God teaches us that none fall so low as those whom privilege has exalted, but who have cared for self rather than right, and for lust more than loyalty to God.

XIII.

GLEANING.

" Where hast thou gleaned to-day ?"—RUTH ii. 19.

THOSE of us who have lived in the country will be familiar with the groups of women and children we have seen coming home laden with grain they have gathered by littles through the long day. Sometimes, as when the weather is constantly wet, it does not pay the poor to go out on this errand, but if the harvest has been a dry time, and the grain left in the fields can be picked up in the same condition that it fell, many of the poor will gather a heap of corn that will, when threshed and sold, buy them a great deal of their winter clothing. There is, however, a great difference nowadays. It is not every farmer who allows the poor a chance. To use Mr. Spurgeon's words, "There are men who would not leave the poor a morsel, and would if possible rake their fields with a small tooth comb." This is not as it should be. God gave His ancient people directions in this matter. "And when ye reap the harvest of your land, thou shalt not make clean riddance of the corners of thy field, when thou reapest, neither shalt thou gather any gleaning of thy harvest; thou shalt leave them unto the poor and to the stranger. I am the Lord your God." On the other hand, the writer has heard a farmer complain that the poor are too indolent to glean, and that it is useless to leave them anything, for they would not pick it up.

God's model farmer, Boaz, said to the reapers, "Let fall some of the handfuls on purpose for her." That looks better than a notice on the gate, scaring the widow and the orphan: "Trespassers will be prosecuted;" the grain will fatten geese and partridges, but bairns are worth more than birds. The fields do not look so tidy with the grain left about, but it would be well for us who are preachers to listen to the voice of Boaz when He bids us "let fall some of the handfuls." There is a story told of an eminent minister that once, when preaching before an association of ministers and deacons, after a most elaborate and beautiful sermon, broke out into exhortation to faith in Jesus, and the acceptance of salvation. This did not belong to the sermon, and it was evident to those who had listened to him that it was something added to his preparation. One of his friends after the service said to him, "Why did you put in that bit of exhortation at the end; your sermon was finished; why tack that on?" "Why," said the good man, "I saw a poor labouring man come in just as I was finishing; he had not heard the sermon, and I could not bear for him not to have anything to carry away."

There are some of my readers whose only chance of obtaining knowledge is by gleaning. Their education has been neglected. Their opportunities of attending a place of worship are few. Their time for reading is limited. In a word, they are not farmers, and can never show a stack: they can only gather by gleaning. To such let me say, GLEAN WHERE THE CORN GROWS AND LIES NEAR AT HAND. It is of no use to go where it is not. You will not find the corn by the wayside, or on the moor. You must go to the fields: it is only on the cultivated land you can find it. And so with the knowledge that is worth possessing. It is not to be found everywhere. For instance, it is not from every pulpit you hear the gospel: Why go where

Christ is not preached? Music will not feed the soul. A beautiful ritual will not satisfy the craving of the heart, nor will rhetoric stop the pangs of hunger. Intellectual preaching, as it is sometimes called, as if gospel preaching could only be done by simpletons, does not, of itself, bind up the broken heart. If your soul is to be fed, go where the bread-corn lies within your reach.

It is not in all company that you may glean wisdom. "He that walketh with wise men shall be wise." To listen to some people's conversation is as profitable as eating chaff, and indeed there are not a few to whom to hearken is to gather poison. How unwise for us to stock our memory with what will prove ammunition or rations for Satan's soldiers, and yet this is sure to be the case if we hearken to the wicked. It would be well for us to bear in mind that we cannot be friendly with the ungodly without storing up some of the talk we hear, and that we thus store sorrow for the future.

It is not every book from which we can glean corn. Books are wide fields: the gates are open, we are welcome to walk about. Have a care, you cannot get rid of what you pick up. Reading a bad book is to gather poison. You must eat what you glean in this way. What would not many Christian men and women give if they could only forget some things they have read! How verses of licentious songs will come up, even amidst psalmody, and unclean jokes will get between the lines of good reading. To the most of us, Where hast thou gleaned? is but another way of saying, What hast thou got as the result of thy life?

To glean successfully WE MUST BE WILLING TO STOOP. Gleaning is stooping. A back that won't bend means a back that will ache for want of food. The woman that means to carry a large burden home must keep her head down all the day. The writer heard a man behind a counter say, "The worst folks to deal with are those who know all you are going to say." This is true enough. A schoolboy who thinks he knows it all is the most hopeless of pupils. The apprentice who will not be told never learns his trade. When the Israelites went out to gather manna, they did not find it hanging by clusters from the tree branches, but on the ground: they must stoop to eat. And is it not so with the bread of life? He who would be fed thereof must humble himself. We may stand, with the Pharisee, and tell of our goodness, but we shall not go down justified. And in the pursuit of knowledge we must be willing to stoop. One reason so many of us are ignorant is, not that knowledge is not to be had, but we don't like people to see us among the learners. We do not care to be seen to stoop! Many a man would have risen if he could have afforded to stoop for awhile. When the eminent missionary, Dr. Milne, first offered for mission work, he was such a rustic that the Committee would not be persuaded he could become a missionary, but one of the members told Dr. Philip that it would perhaps be worth while to send him out as a servant to the mission. Dr. Philip spoke to Milne aside on this proposal, and asked him if he would consent. With a smile, the future eminent man said, "Certainly, to be a hewer of wood is too great an honour for me when the Lord's house is building." So, by stooping, he rose to be the great man whom God honoured so much in China.

If we would glean a heap, we must be content with A LITTLE AT A TIME. The woman who has gathered the largest bundle of corn never once picked up a handful. It was mostly in single ears. "Here a little, and there a little." It is wonderful what may be done by never passing by a thing that is worth preserving. To note down, every day, each remarkable thing, would make a wonderful volume in time. To do this thoroughly, we must know the value of each grain of truth. In our own experience it is not the sermon that has been effective, but some one thought on it, and that perhaps some very simple thing. How much comfort we have obtained from some line of a hymn! Or perhaps some simple anecdote has done what the effort of the preacher had failed to accomplish.

It would be well for us to pick up all that is worth gleaning. We have trampled under foot during our lives that which, if saved, would have done much to make a golden old age for ourselves. What waste of thought there is for want of care for the littles! Much goes to the manure heap that might have made muscle and fibre.

If any young folks do me the honour of reading this, be advised to pick up every good thing that comes within reach, and don't let the thought that it is only a little prevent your stooping, for stacks are made up of single straws, and London is made up of single houses, which were built a brick at a time.

No one can glean well who is not ABLE TO PERSEVERE. Gleaning is tiring work. It means a back-ache. Whenever we see a bundle of corn on a gleaner's head, we know she must have stooped thousands of times. None but those who have done it know how hard it is to glean that which is to be of any use. The poor must not give up because they are tired; and this holds good in many things, besides working in the fields. We must, if we mean to succeed, be willing to go on long after we are weary. We cannot expect to have it all our own way. If we were as willing to spur ourselves to perseverance as we are to urge on our weary horses, we should accomplish much more than we do. Abraham Lincoln was asked if he thought the war would be over while he was President. "Can't say, sir." "But, Mr. Lincoln, what do you mean to do?" "Peg away, sir,—keep pegging away." And pegging away liberated millions of bondmen, and wiped the foul stain of slavery from America's scutcheon.

> "Many strokes, tho' with a little axe,
> Hew down and fell the hardest timbered oak."

If we would lay up riches in bags that do not grow old, and store in the place where thieves do not break through nor steal, we must keep at it, not stopping because some one else says his back aches, so he shall stop; perhaps if he heard us say, "My back aches too, but I shall keep on," he would be shamed to perseverance.

We shall glean with greater care and industry if we remember that we must live for ever on the results of this life. What we gather in this world will make our heaven the brighter, or our hell the darker. If men did but think they gather gold for a crown, or iron for fetters, they would be more careful what they pick up. We read that Ruth "beat out what she had gleaned." All we have done will be threshed, and every one shall

"EAT OF THE FRUIT OF THEIR OWN WAY."

XIV.

"*VIRTUE IS GONE OUT OF ME.*"

LUKE viii. 46.

IT has been well said, "The fashion of this world passeth away," for even language changes its meaning, and words cease to have the same significance they once had. Virtue at one time meant strength. Now it is used to denote purity. Jesus meant that power had gone out from Him. It is worth while to note that virtue cannot leave one and pass to another without a loss to the giver. There can be little doubt that the sacred body of Jesus had to suffer for being the medium of healing, and that very costly was the honour of being the shrine of Divinity.

It is no wonder that some of the most effective of preachers have had worn and wasted bodies, as the tax for being able to give so much strength to others. Whenever you listen to a man who lifts you up, and from whose words you derive energy which enables you to battle with your difficulties, make sure that the preacher has to pay for it, in a wearied and worn body. We read in one place, "Jesus, therefore, being wearied with His journey, sat thus on the well." He appears to have been too fatigued to go into the town. His disciples were not too weary, but then, as they came along they had not to give out power and grace. Perhaps one reason why Jesus had to toil in His early life as a carpenter, was to invigorate His frame, and fit it for the three years of waste which lay between the baptism at Jordan and the cross of Calvary.

Virtue is gone out of me to ONE WHO FAILED TO GET HELP ELSEWHERE. We are told that the poor woman spoken of here had been ill for twelve long years. During that time she had gone from one medical man to another, but without finding relief. She had "suffered many things of many physicians, and was nothing bettered, but rather grew worse." "Had spent all her living upon physicians, neither could be healed of any." As a last resource, she came and tried Jesus. Is she not a picture of many among us, who try everything but the right thing, and also go anywhere rather than to the Saviour? Have we not many vile impostors who rival Christ, and who profess to give peace to the soul without reference to the atonement? What quackery!

Have any of my readers gone to others rather than to the Great Physician? Very likely, for men don't like the terms of Jesus. He charges nothing, but demands that we should go nowhere else. And we are so fond of paying. If only Jesus would let men bring ever so little of works, He would have many more patients. What doctor have you been to? There are many of them. Let me warn you against some of them.

There is DR. MERRYMAN. He has a very large practice. He is the most popular of all the soul doctors, and has an amazingly large connection among young people. If some one goes to him complaining of a sad heart, he will prescribe a change. "You must have some light reading. You must not read the Bible any more, at least, till you are better. That book is all very well for old people, and those who are going to die, but you, my dear sir, will live many years, and, I trust, happy years, that is, if you will but take my prescriptions." By-and-by the patient returns. "No better, doctor, worse if anything." "Ah! you must go to the theatre, attend the opera, and see some comedy." "I have tried that, and it did me no good."

"Well, well, Christmas is coming, and we must try a little dancing. You want some gay society, you will soon dance away that gloom. And in the meantime, be very careful what place of worship you attend. Beware of those preachers who will frighten you by talking of God's anger against sin. Attend some place where there is respectable society, and nice music, and a short sermon—*that* will soothe you. You will soon be better," etc., etc.

There is another of these impudent quacks. I mean DR. DEVOTEE, who, like the famous Mr. Merryman, has a large number of patients, but they are generally rather older; indeed, many of them have been under Merryman till they were tired out; then they have gone over to the other side of the way to try if Devotee could help them. If you go into his waiting room, you will see some who have had disappointments, blighted affections, etc. When you are shown into his room, you notice how very grave he is,—none of the flippancy of the other, he does not approve of Merryman's prescriptions. "He did not understand your case, my dear madam. You need severe treatment, you must have strong medicine. I shall prescribe a course of fasting and prayer. It would have done you good to have gone with those who have just set off on a pilgrimage. You are weary of the frivolity of the world. If you don't get better soon, you shall enter a religious order, become a nun, and spend the remainder of your life in the retreat of innocence and sanctity, and behind the high wall be sheltered from evil."

There is yet another of these medical gentlemen you must look in upon. This is where DR. APATHY lives. He is the favourite doctor among men of business and commerce. They will tell you, "Merryman is all very well for the youngsters, and

Devotee suits the women, but for a sensible practical man, commend me to Apathy. Bless you, what I suffered before I went to him! I could not sleep at nights for thinking I might lose my soul. Really business began to suffer; so I went to him, and he soon put me to rights. When I told him my symptoms, he said, 'I understand you, my dear fellow, you need a sedative. Stick to your newspaper, and give up all that nonsense about family prayer. Have a game of whist in the evening, and an extra glass of grog. Try to sleep as much as you can during the sermon, and if you cannot manage that, try to arrange your next day's business, so that after that you can dine and sleep away Sunday.' And what has been the result? Why, I have never any of those queer feelings about death and the judgment day. I am all right."

Do you know, dear reader, any of these men? You will not get a cure with them;

"*VIRTUE IS GONE OUT OF ME.*" 161

they will deceive you, take your money, and then desert you at the last. If you have been vainly trying to get a cure at the wrong place, come to Jesus, and He will save you.

" None but Jesus
Can do wretched sinners good."

Virtue has gone out of me to ONE WHO HAS OVERCOME GREAT DIFFICULTIES.

This poor woman must have found it very difficult to come to Christ, for at least two reasons. She was ceremoniously unclean. What! go to Jesus, the great Prophet, when I am not fit to touch any one? Yes, I will go to Him, and try His skill, and see if He will reject me? Does the thought of your sins scare you from Jesus? The more unfit for heaven, the greater the reason for coming to Christ. The worse you are, the more welcome to Jesus. Don't lose time trying to cure yourself, or to mitigate the symptoms. Come away to Jesus at once. If you were seized with cholera, and knew of some doctor who had never lost a cholera patient, you would not wait till the symptoms were a little less violent. How well known, but never worn out, are the lines of the hymn,—

> "If you tarry till you're better
> You will never come at all."

Don't lose any more time; you have lost enough already, as this poor woman seems to have done. She had delayed until it was almost too late. She came *behind* Him. If she had waited much longer she would have died as she was. Come behind. "Better late than never."

There was the difficulty of the crowd. The people thronged Him; and no wonder, for He was on His way to heal the ruler's daughter. The crowd was between her and the Lord. Aye, and it is so yet. Very often we find the friends and admirers of Christ keeping away some who seek His face. Let none of us make that blunder. Do not stand

"VIRTUE IS GONE OUT OF ME." 163

between the sinner and the Saviour. Is not this the sin of priestcraft? Do not many, well-meaning men, it may be, hide Christ by their ceremonies? Is not this the sin of a narrow theology?—those who are delighted to speak of the "little flock." Have not some preachers sinned against the penitent, if not against Christ, by giving eloquence instead of gospel?

But the woman persevered. She could not get at Jesus to tell Him all she could have said; but she touched Him, and so we find Him saying, "Virtue is gone out of me." Does the soul sincerely seeking Jesus ever fail? It is our hope for those devout ones who sit under a Christless ministry, and who cannot come near, yet touch as it were the hem of the garment. It is yet true that as many as touched were made whole of whatever disease they had.

Virtue has gone out of me to ONE WHO HAS FAITH.

As the poor woman thought of the crowd, she felt she had not the strength to force her way; but she said, "If I may but touch." This was not the first time a touch had been mighty. She had heard of it, and believed, and argued, "Why should He not heal me as well as they?" Is there, among the readers of this book, one who is in distress about his soul? say, Why should I not be saved? God does not show partiality. He forgives all who rest on the atonement. Put down this book, dear reader, and kneel down, and look away to Jesus. Exercise faith in Jesus just this moment. I should like some soul to be made happy in Jesus while reading this. Why should you not be saved? Did not Jesus suffer in your stead? Have not your sins been punished? Then rest upon the fact that Christ is your Substitute, and rejoice in Him who died to redeem you. Don't talk of setting aside a future time for fasting and prayer. Come to Jesus, just now.

Do not wait till you have altered this, or improved that, all that can be done afterwards. If this poor woman had a part of a bottle of medicine left in the house, she did not say, I will go home and finish the bottle, and then come to Jesus. She did better; she said, "If I may but touch His clothes, I shall be made whole."

Virtue is gone out of me to one WHO MUST CONFESS THE TRUTH.

Jesus did not allow the woman to keep her secret. Doubtless, as soon as she found the cure, her heart would be filled with love to Him who had made her whole; but, poor timid thing, she would fain have gone home, and told nobody in the crowd. Who touched me? Master, why do you ask? many an one in the crowd is touching Thee. Who does not touch Thee? so said the disciples. "Virtue is gone out of me." He looked about, and caught the woman's eye, who now had strength to press through the multitude and fall down close to His feet, and tell Him all the truth.

Timid disciple, have you derived benefit from Jesus, and yet have not owned to it? Secret lover of Jesus, take up the cross, tell the story of thy deliverance. It will be all the better for thee. If Jesus had allowed the woman to have returned home, she would have been the loser. She might have doubted if the cure was permanent; but now that she has heard Him say, "Daughter, be of good comfort, thy faith hath made thee whole," she can rejoice in the knowledge of a complete deliverance. And if you want assurance, confess what you feel of the grace of God. Let the world hear you tell the truth, and you shall hear Him say, "Be of good comfort."

One other word before you shut the book. Be not satisfied to be among the crowd that press round Jesus and touch Him, without being any the better for it. *God forbid that you should be in the crowd, and yet that concerning you He should not say,—*

"VIRTUE IS GONE OUT OF ME!"

XV.

STONING THE GODS.

"*Once was I stoned.*"—ACTS xiv.; 2 COR. xi. 25.

THAT is no ordinary heap of stones. See, there is blood on the sharp-edged ones, and skin, and hair! And no common blood. It is the blood of one of earth's best sons. Whose blood is it? The blood of Paul, Christ's missionary. We saw another heap twelve years ago, on which was the blood of Stephen. Only a dozen years between the man who held the clothes of Stephen's murderers, and the martyr Paul, for he was a martyr then in intention, and for anything we know he literally died for the truth. For he tells us, "Whether in the body or out of the body I cannot tell." Persecutors may become helpers, and he who, wolf like, made havoc among the flock of Christ, may lay down his life for the sheep. This book may fall into the hands of some foe of Jesus and the gospel. You, my friend, may yet become one of the advocates of the truth you hate so much. Yes, the pirate may yet carry lawful cargo. Do you wish it were so? Then haul down your ensign and run up the colours of God the King, the white flag and red cross. Cease to do evil, learn to do well. Cast yourself on the mercy of God, and instead of execution for rebellion and piracy, you shall be the commander of your own vessel, and be used to run emigrants over to the land of holiness and beauty, where He waits to house them for ever.

"Sermons in stones." Yes, there are many homilies in such a blood-stained stone-heap as this, in every pebble and boulder. As we turn them over, they say, HOWEVER GOOD A MAN IS HIS MISTAKES WILL INJURE HIM. Being godly does not insure infallibility. Paul made several mistakes in his life, and there seems to have been one here. It is not very easy to account for the sudden revulsion of feeling; the people at first thought they were the gods come down in the likeness of men. Afterward, Paul was stoned by the same people. Some light is incidentally here thrown on the personal appearance of these heroic men. Barnabas was called Jupiter, so we conclude he was a massive, fine-looking man, while Paul was Mercury, whom we know from the ancient statues of that god was always represented as a small-limbed, slightly-built man. While we may not be able altogether to account for the sudden change in the feelings of the people towards these two men, we may see that there need have been no mistaking them for gods. Paul did not use the common formula when he healed the cripple. It was not "*In the name of Jesus of Nazareth,* rise up and walk," but, "Stand upright on thy feet!" We quite think that Paul meant no harm, but it was misleading to the poor ignorant heathen, and he had to smart for it. How much better if the bystanders had been led to ask, Who is the god they invoked? Who is this Jesus of Nazareth? It is a new name to us: who is it? Let not your good be evil spoken of. Avoid the appearance of evil. Oh, if we could be spared the mistakes of good men! Because punishment and suffering come to the good if they blunder. Here is a man who is anxious to give money, and so sees what he thinks is a good thing, and recklessly ventures more than he can afford, and so you have "another of these Christians sold up!" The father of a family, so much engaged in church work that he cannot be ever at home, and so the boys run wild. "What plagues they are! I do believe good men's children are the worst of all," the neighbours say. Zeal runs away with another, and without thinking of health, he is worn out. If men forget they are human, the kind of work they do won't prevent their wearing out, and so there is a gap in the ranks before the time. Perhaps, if the truth was told, many a one has been martyred because he could not be quiet, and it may be some of my readers are suffering, not for conscience' sake, but for the want of common sense!

But do not these stones teach us THE WAY THE WORLD USES ITS BENEFACTORS? Stone the man who healed the cripple! That is the way we always do. We do not deny that the cripple has been healed, but stone him. What business has he to do anything new? Does not the world often starve its geniuses? Who expects wealth for an inventor? You must be content to be the ladder up which other people rise in the world, if you have seen further than anyone else, and are bringing out something fresh. The history of poets and painters tells us of hunger and nakedness. Some of the books that live were written in naked garrets, and others in prison cells. Livingstone has done more to make England famous than most men, and yet he was more than poor, and the expedition that found him was sent out by America. It was the star and stripes that mingled with the Union Jack at Ugiji. Do not complain, my friend, if the world hate you. Don't expect gratitude if you are doing good. You will be better off than God if you get thanks for kindness. Why should we be surprised? Look at the cross. Who hangs between the malefactors? What crime has He done? What are the people crucifying Him for? Feeding the hungry? Opening the eyes of the blind? Making lame men independent of crutches? Raising the dead? What, has He done all this? Has He always spoken kindly to the erring, and helped many to be good,—then crucify Him? Away with Him; He is not fit to live! The servant is not above his Lord. If the Master went this way, why should not the servant? Bishop Hall once said, "Let who will hope to walk on roses and violets to the glory of heaven; O Saviour, let me trace Thee by the track of Thy blood; and by Thy red steps follow Thee to Thine eternal rest and happiness!"

There are many texts in this stone-heap. Here is one. BIGOTRY BRUTALIZES IGNORANCE. "Certain Jews persuaded the people." You have the history of persecution epitomized in that nineteenth verse. Bigotry makes a tool of ignorance. The priests have pulled the strings before to-day, and are trying to get hold of them now. Let us beware of ignorance. Education has always been the foe of priestcraft. But let us not content ourselves with our children learning everything but the Word of God. It is no good sign that doctrinal preaching is on the decrease, that, in fact, the people do not like to be instructed, which means they are making themselves fit tools for the priest. Popery has no chance so long as the Bible is understood by the people; but let us cease to learn the truth, and no longer be able "to give an answer to every man that asketh you a reason of the hope that is in you," and we shall become puppets for priestcraft.

If you are not ignorant, and so cannot become brutal, do not be a bigot. Do not fear new ideas. It is true they did not occur to you, but let another man explore the realms of thought, if you do not care to leave your quiet home. There will be quite enough to throw stones at the man with a new idea without your throwing one.

If a man loves God, he has been promised "a crown of life," and you will not like, should you see him crowned, to think of the time when you threw a stone at his head! Religion will not save you from bigotry; there are no bigots like religious ones. What hard names are used by very religious men when they speak of some whom they think not so liberal as themselves, all because they say God will punish sin eternally. Let us learn to tolerate the man who loves God, seeing that we shall have to live with him for ever. Whatever liberty we claim for ourselves, give another man the same, and let not London see what Lystra saw,—men who worship Jehovah stir up others to injure a man who prays to the same God as themselves.

But all the stones are not bloody. Does not that teach, PERSECUTION IS LIMITED IN ITS RESULTS? "Once was I stoned." Paul lived twenty years after this, but never was stoned again. The enemy had tried to do it before, but was not able. "Once was *I* stoned," not Barnabas. God did not put him to the trial. Not the other disciples, only Paul. I was stoned, not killed; at least, though left for dead, I rose up and came into the city. It may be that dark days are coming for the Church of God. It may be that many may have to suffer, but the foes of God cannot slay Him. They may beat out our brains, but they cannot kill the truth.

Paul did not give up the work to which he was called because he had to suffer. No, brave little man, we see him just as the disciples stood around him, weeping over his poor body, and preparing to bury it; he opens his eyes, and, though weak and sore, stands up and comes into Lystra again, and "preached the gospel to that city." Here was good for evil. Mark how the Christian hero makes his very sufferings useful, telling the Church at Lystra, and every scar illustrated the truth that "we must through much tribulation enter into the kingdom of God." This was not the last time he visited the place; once more he went, and found fruit remaining, and became acquainted with his son in the gospel, Timothy. How true it is that the blood of the martyr is the seed of the church. Such men as the friend and comforter of Paul, as Timothy was, are cheap at such a price. Let us trust our God, even when we are hurt in doing good; out of our wounds there may flow that which shall heal many. 'Tis still true what Herbert sang,—

> "Tempests are calm to Thee, they know Thy hand,
> And hold it fast, as children do their father's,
> Which cry and follow."

XVI.

THE HISTORY OF A LETTER.

"And Hezekiah received the letter of the hand of the messengers, and read it: and Hezekiah went up into the house of the Lord, and spread it before the Lord."—2 KINGS xix. 14.

HOW easy to say, "the letter;" and yet, how much the words may mean! The postman, as he goes his rounds, would become the most melancholy of men if he thought much upon the budget he carries. To some houses joy, to others misery,—nay, to the same house joy treads on the heels of sorrow, or *vice versa*. We don't know what to-morrow may bring us; the postman's knock may be the knell of doom or the signal for peals of joyous laughter.

What a letter was that which Hezekiah

received! In form it would be very different to our ideas of a letter. The Assyrians did not use paper, or even skins, but did their writing on clay. You may see, in the British Museum, a conveyance of land, written, not on parchment, but on clay, and then baked hard. So it is very likely that the letter was a tablet of terra cotta. It has been thought by some that Rabshakeh was the writer of these railing letters. This renegade Jew, like most apostates, gloried in his shame. He was a master of coarse invective, and could say things never to be forgotten. For instance, when he sneered at Hezekiah for depending upon Egypt, and compared that nation to one of the papyrus reeds which grow on the banks of the Nile, —to lean upon it was to break it, and have it pierce the hand. In the letter, he told the king of Israel that he would share the fate of the other nations whom Sennacherib had destroyed, and told him to

THE HISTORY OF A LETTER. 181

note that the gods of those nations had not delivered them; and even goes to the length of suggesting that Jehovah was cheating the pious king, when encouraging him to believe that He was greater than Assyria. The letter winds up by asking Hezekiah to think what had become of other crowned heads, and suggesting that soon he would join the company of those who had been degraded by Assyria.

This was trouble, but it was trouble that might have been prevented. Hezekiah ought never to have paid tribute to Sennacherib. When first the demand was made, he should have called on the name of the Lord. In 2 Kings xviii. we read that Hezekiah prayed to be delivered: but he prayed to the king of Assyria. To stave off the threatened destruction, he had to cut off the gold from the doors of the temple. It was all lost. The greedy monarch was not to be thus satisfied; he meant having all the wealth that

Solomon had accumulated. Let us learn to *never submit to the claims of sin.* We can never satisfy it. Much will have more. Sin, like Sennacherib, will take all you will give, and then come for more, and when it has got all it will come for you. The devil has no right to a penny of our money, or a moment of our time. If we could have in the treasury of the Lord the tribute good people are paying to Satan, we should be able to carry on much of the Lord's work that languishes for funds. Young men and women, let me say to you, Never give way to the claims of sin. If you submit once, you will have to submit again, until hell will talk of "vested interests" in your time and money!

WHAT DID HEZEKIAH DO WITH THE LETTER? He did not send a hasty answer. Many a quarrel might have been prevented if men would spread disagreeable letters before the Lord. Many a family feud would never have been brought about but for the want of this. If you get letters that give you pain, before you pen a reply send a message to God, and He will teach you to indite what may turn away wrath.

He did not send to Egypt; he was cured of that now. If some one who reads this is in trouble, let me counsel you to remember what is a command as well as a promise, "Call upon me in the day of trouble." Far too many of us treat God as though He had no existence. We try everybody else before going to the Lord. We can quack with our small ailments, but when we feel in danger we call in the men of skill, forgetting that the cold may be the prelude to a fever, and that little trials are sometimes opening the way for larger ones. Hezekiah did now what he ought to have done at the first. What a great deal of trouble he might have saved himself if, at the first appearance of the Assyrian army, he had gone to the house of the Lord to pray: then he would have been saved the necessity of going there to cut off the gold from the doors. The right thing is always best, and in the long run the cheapest.

"*Went up into the house of the Lord.*" Where was he so likely to find God as in His house? The writer knew a pious and intelligent widow who had a great deal of trial, and who assured him that she was never in perplexity but she was sure to be guided to the right conclusion as she sat in chapel. Something either in the sermon, or lesson, or prayer, or hymn would tell her what to do.

> "In every new distress
> Will to His house repair;
> Will think upon His wondrous grace,
> And seek deliverance there."

Hezekiah did not hear God reproach him for going elsewhere first. There is much force in the promise, "If any of you lack wisdom, let him ask of God, that giveth to all men liberally and *upbraideth not.*" Perhaps you have tried everybody else, and are almost ashamed to go to God now. Do not fear but He will treat you as kindly as He did Hezekiah.

Have you noticed the prayer of the king, how he speaks of God as dwelling between the cherubim? Maybe he had heard how Sennacherib sat on his throne between winged bulls and lions; but he had heard Isaiah tell of seeing the Lord surrounded by winged intelligences. The great stone images which stood on either side of the throne of Assyria were enough to terrify those who stood before the king: but they could not move. God had only to speak to His winged messenger, and the angel was gone to crush the foes of Jehovah and His people.

It is a model prayer; not like many, which must try the patience of God, going all round the world, instead of fastening upon the thing needed, and asking for that. If our prayers were more like telegrams we should have speedier answers. One of the best prayers the writer ever heard of was put up by a man who had been awakened at some special service; it was in these words: "Lord, save me from the public house, for it has been my ruin!" The prayer of the pious king appealed to God for the sake of His honour—"*that all the kingdoms of the earth may know that Thou art the Lord God.*" How the Almighty is touched by an appeal of this sort. If we thought more of God's honour in our prayers, we should be more often answered. It is said of Sammy Hick that on one occasion he had been led to pray in the congregation for rain, and after he left the chapel, and had reached the house, he seemed very uneasy, and kept going to the door and looking out. Some one asked him what was the matter? "Didn't thou hear me pray for rain? What will these infidels say if they know that I prayed for it and God didn't send it?" Such jealousy for God was not and cannot ever be in vain.

WAS THE LETTER EVER ANSWERED? Yes, for Jehovah answered it Himself. He did not trouble Hezekiah to do it; and the answer is worthy of the Lord. How he reproves the pride and annoyance of the king of Assyria—"Whom hast thou reproached and blasphemed?" In Isaiah x. we find other allusions to the threat of Sennacherib; the prophet spoke the feeling of God, and encouraged the fainting hearts of the people of God. But the answer never was sent to the Assyrian. God did not condescend to reply to him personally. He may have thought that His message had so dismayed Hezekiah that in a very short time there would be an ambassage desiring peace, and offering abject submission. We know what the result was, and how suddenly the bolt of vengeance struck down the proud blasphemer. Is it not the same to-day? Are not many of those who lift themselves up against the Lord doomed in the same way? God does not condescend to send an answer to their proud boastings, but He has replied, and could they but know what He has spoken, they would be in abject terror.

While nothing appears to have been said to the foe, the friends of Jehovah were much comforted by the reply to the letter. Jerusalem is represented as a Jewish maiden, laughing Assyria to scorn. Yes, when God laughs we may. It would help us more if we cultivated sacred mirth. Why should the enemy be the only one to smile? "He laughs best who laughs last," says the old proverb, but he who knows that he will laugh last, should laugh all the way through. God will win the day; then let none of us who are on His side whine and cry, but rejoice in the Lord, and in merriment sing psalms. The twenty-eighth verse in this chapter used to be a puzzle to students of the Bible, but since the marbles have been dug up, we learn from them that it was the custom of the wicked kings of Assyria to do to men after this cruel fashion. One of the sculptures which portray the history of Assyria shows three poor captives brought into the presence of the king with a cord through their lips and nose! So, "I will put my hook in thy nose, and my bridle in thy lips, and turn thee back." Are any of my readers sorely tempted of the evil one? Does he threaten to swallow you up? Laugh at him, and tell him that Jehovah can turn him back as easily as He did Sennacherib.

There is a POSTSCRIPT TO GOD'S ANSWER (see verse 35).—"It came to pass that night—they were all dead corpses"! Fancy if you saw in the newspaper to-morrow, "Sudden death of 185,000 soldiers!" What a stir it would make! What a sight the camp must have been next morning. There has been much discussion as to how it happened. There is no mention of it in the Assyrian record. They were ready enough to boast, but when Sennacherib crept back to his palace, he did not instruct the historian to chronicle his disgrace. Herodotus tells us that the Egyptians, against whom Sennacherib was then at war, ascribed the destruction of their foes to the power of their gods. There has been considerable discussion amongst the learned as to the cause of the destruction of so large an army, and it is generally understood now to have been the simoon. Cambyses, king of the Medes, lost 50,000 men by one of these dreadful winds. But whether the wind was the messenger, or whether an angel had the wind in his power, it matters not; we read of "stormy wind fulfilling His word." God willed it, and nature hasted to do His bidding.

Sennacherib does not appear to have been

with the main army, and so escaped for the time; but vengeance followed him home. Let us pause and contrast the two kings mentioned in this story, and we shall see the difference between the friends and foes of God. Look at Hezekiah. Though he made mistakes, he was a sincere, good man; he meant right, and so in the day of distress could seek the Lord. Look at him in the house of God. He is in great trouble; He bows before the Lord. See, some one is coming! it is the prophet. What is the message? Will God reproach me for not coming before? Will He refuse now to help us? Listen, thus saith the Lord. "That which thou hast prayed to me against Sennacherib king of Assyria I have heard." Now look at the enemy of God when he was in trouble. He, too, is in trouble, he has not prospered, and so will seek the help of his god. Tradition says that he intended to offer up two of his sons as human sacrifices. He is in the house of his god, seeking aid, when a step is heard: how quietly the men walk; there are two of them; they steal behind the worshipping monarch, they pierce him with their knives; and, as he looks upon them with his dying gaze, he sees that those he intended to offer to his god have been his death! "The light of the righteous rejoiceth, but the lamp of the wicked shall be put out."

XVII.

WORKING FOR THE KING.

"*With the king for his work.*"—1 CHRON. iv. 23.

WHAT a chapter this is for hard names! A preacher looking for a text here would feel like a lad seeking blackberries in a thorn hedge; nearly every verse bristles with words difficult to pronounce; yet here and there we have a sweet verse or two, with some beautiful lesson for the people of God. Let not our young readers hesitate about searching these dry chapters which seem but a register of names, for now and then they will come upon some lovely jewel imbedded in the shale of genealogy that will well pay them for their toil.

For instance, in the ninth and tenth verses, we have the story of Jabez, or, to put his name into English, Sorrowful. It was a strange name, but his mother was determined to perpetuate the memory of some grief she had when the lad was born,—something that touched more nearly than the joy of her son's birth. It may be that there was war at the time, and that her husband was killed, or the house burned, so the child was to be the remembrancer of evil days. But of all her children, none gave her so much pleasure, and we can fancy how the neighbours would praise Sorrowful when he began to walk, and talk of his sweet smile. Ah, there is none like Sorrowful! By-and-bye he came to manhood, and then, when farmers had to fight amidst their grain, and drive back the foe from the harvest-field, none were so brave as the child of woe, and we can fancy the women saying to his mother, " Sorrowful has done the best of all." Would not his mother wish she had given him some other name? And shall it not be so with our sorrows? As they work out some exceeding weight of glory, shall we not sing the sweetest about the very things which on earth made us to shed the most tears? Sorrowful is most honourable!

Again, in the eighteenth verse we read of a woman who is called Bithiah; very little is said of her, but her name is most significant. She was the child of Pharaoh. Which Pharaoh? Was she the daughter of the man who opposed the God of Israel? Did the actions of the illustrious man whom she had saved from the river lead her to look at her own position and choose like Moses to suffer affliction with the people of God? Of that we are not sure, but of this we are certain, that a daughter of Pharaoh called herself "daughter of Jehovah," for that is the meaning of Bithiah; suggesting that we should never think any family hopeless, for God gets Himself honour in various ways, and sometimes by saving some one whose name seems a curse. The writer thought so the other day when he saw advertised, "Why am I a Christian?" by W. Bradlaugh.

Towards the end of the chapter, we read of some whose prosperity was their ruin. "Fat pasture and good" was their lot, but there were those who were on the look out for some place to settle, so seeing this desirable pasture they slew the shepherds who had had it in possession for so long; teaching us that the more we have the more likely we are to be robbed, and that what makes our lot desirable may awaken envy and covetousness in others, and even riches may bring destruction.

The twenty-third verse suggests ideas worth consideration. "These were the potters, and those that dwelt among plants and hedges: there they dwelt with the king for his work." Do you note how WORK LINKS MEN TO KINGS, for you have potters, gardeners, and hedgers mixed up with the king. There are many wrong ideas in the world about labour. It would not be right, perhaps, but my pen had almost written, Work is the only respectable thing. And yet not a few people try to bring up their children to do without, and you will see a man toil early and late to make money, getting no enjoyment out of it for himself, for he pinches himself to save; and when you get at the reason, it is that he may make his son a gentleman, which means, someone who can live without work. This is not according to the Divine idea, for we find Jesus saying, "My Father worketh hitherto, and I work." Is not the Creator ever designing some new form of beauty, and giving delight to the children of men by some new manifestation of Divine taste and industry? It is not for nothing that Christ, the wisdom of God, toiled at the carpenter's bench, and was as much the Son of God when He stood up to His ankles in shavings, as when He walked the seas. The apostles were men whose physical power had been developed by labour, and were used to toil before they began to preach. Indeed, if you take out of the Bible all the stories of men who worked for their living, you will rob it of its greatest beauty, and do us a terrible wrong.

If some boy does me the honour to read this, let me tell him that the producers are the wealth of a nation. The men and women who work, whether with brain or hand, or both, are the people who save the nation from ruin. It matters not whether you paint a picture, or beat out a horse shoe : labour is wealth, and no shower fertilizes the earth like the sweat of honest toilers. Make something, then; ideas or bricks, it matters not, only let there be something in existence at night that was not in the morning. That which makes Longfellow's village blacksmith worth singing about is :—

> "Each morning sees some task begun,
>   Each evening sees it close;
> Something attempted, something done,
>   Has earned a night's repose."

Is it not so in Christian life and experience? What is a man's religion worth if it does not teach him to labour? Are we not to work out our salvation, and that for the best of reasons, "It is God that worketh in us"? The sunshine and rain are useless to the fields that have not been tilled. He who has no plough needs not to trouble to sharpen his scythe. Bibles and sermons to the idle are not, cannot be appreciated, and Sabbaths are but weariness to the man who does no kind of Christian work. Do not mistake yourself for a Christian because you like some popular preacher: it is on the same principle that wasps like honey, but they will starve rather than make it; and some of these sermon-hunters come to steal what they could not earn.

You would not have heard of these men if they had not worked. Their toil has bound up their life with the king's life. Why should you not act so that the story of God cannot be fully told without your name being mentioned? Have you been at ease in Zion? then rouse yourself. Oh, you who are on strike, think what you are losing, and what, perhaps, is worse, how much you are causing the King to lose! He is taking on fresh hands to-day, and He will not turn the old hands back if only He sees that you mean work.

There is another idea which grows out of this, and that is, KINGS NEED DIFFERENT KINDS OF WORKERS. If the monarch wanted a flower, he must have a gardener to grow it; if he broke a dish, he could not make another. God needs us, not that He could not have done without us, but He has elected to win the world by human instrumentality, and, let it be said with reverence, the interests of God are very greatly bound up with the progress of humanity. If His Church is indolent, His cause suffers. If the Church is on the alert, then His interests are cared for. There is a sense in which God needs us, and cannot carry out His plans without us. It is easy to see that He will not convert the world without the Church's co-operation.

Both gardeners and potters are needed by the king; there is great variety in the kinds of work, so that various types of skill are necessary. Whatever your talent, there is room for you. Not only genius, but dogged drudgery. We want the artist to paint the picture, and the workman to frame it; the author to write the book, and the printer to give it to the world. Perhaps you would rather be a gardener than a potter. It is cleaner. Yes, it is, but the potter has not the same worry and anxiety the gardener has. The artizan knows when his work is done for the day; the clay will be in the morning where he left it last night; but the flower, will that be there? Has not the wind changed? The breeze that has come over the barren steppes of Tartary carries death to fragile beauty, and the gardener wakes, while the potter rests, for what is the east wind to him? Frost, blight, worms, drought—these cannot hurt clay, but they ruin flowers; and so, in proportion to the beauty of the material, must be the anxiety of the worker. Do I hear some one say, When I was taken into the garden, I had hoped to have worked amongst the flowers, but I have been set to plant hedges and keep them in order? Well, do you not see that your work is of untold value to the man whose place is to produce flowers for the King's table? You are growing a leafy wall, that shall barricade those things of beauty, and screen them from the breath of the destroyer. Only a mother;

nothing to do for God but to nurse children. Ah, but if you do it well, shall not your boy sing in heaven how his mother's life shielded him from harm and kept his soul alive?

Are you, my reader, one of those spoken of as "these are the potters"? Is yours the lowly task to sit at the wheel, or to stand amid the soot of the baking clay? Dirty, grimy work, you say. Yes, it is, but the gardener is dependent upon you. Does he want to send in a choice rose he has just cut? Does he wish his rose to stand on the King's table? then he must have your help. He must ask for one of your vases. How true it is that no one man can do all that needs to be done, even with his own gifts. The man of scholarly mind, who is able to translate from the original, is not always gifted with the power of speech, and may not be as able to catch the ear of the multitude as some unlettered, but eloquent enthusiast. Many a warrior, O potter, shall drink out of thy clay pitcher, and, refreshed, shall go back to the field to win new honours for his sovereign. The treasure, so heavenly in its origin, is kept in "earthen vessels." The gardener must come to thee for pitchers to water his plants. It may not be known out of what pitcher the water came which saved the plant in the days of drought. There was a time when that plant of renown men call John Bunyan was in peril. You remember when he had given up blasphemy, and had become a Pharisee, instead of the tap-room he frequented churches, and was well-nigh eaten up with spiritual pride. To see him come out of church, puffed up with the thought of his goodness, evidently feeling that he was an apprentice-angel, and soon to be out of his time! the devil was surer of him than when his mouth was full of filthy blasphemies. But one day, as he came down Bedford streets, with his soldering-iron, he overheard some godly women speaking of grace in the heart. He had thought of taking part, but when he heard them speak of human righteousness as filthy rags, he felt they spake an unknown tongue. But God's grace came to him that day. We have all enjoyed the perfume of the heavenly plant, but no one knows the names of the three women who were but pitchers from the King's potteries; the water they held, though, was that of life, and brought the precious gift to Bunyan!

There they dwelt with the king.—Willing to stay in His service all "the days of their appointed time." Let us be willing to stay. Heaven will keep. Some day we shall go to dwell with the King in another sense. As one looks round the workshops and gardens of the king, we miss some who were wont to toil there. They are gone. Yes, gone from the soot of the pottery, and the burning heat of the garden, to dwell "in quietness and assurance for ever."

XVIII.

ROPES AND RAGS.

JEREMIAH xxxviii.

ONE of the things one learns by living in London is, that all the grand things are not in the broad streets. Down some of the narrow and unfrequented paths we now and then drop upon a bit of quaint beauty, in the way of architecture or window gardening; or, it may be, that in some back street we pass an old-fashioned shop window, in which are treasures of art and skill that tempt one to break the tenth commandment. And, more or less so, it is the same with the highways and byways of Holy Scripture. Jeremiah will never be the popular prophet that Isaiah is; he is not read with the same delight and frequency; yet there are passages of wondrous beauty in his prophecy, and now and then scenes of great dramatic power, such as this chapter contains.

The story is very remarkable. It is at a time of great terror. The din of war is at the gates of Jerusalem. The proud king of Babylon, who goes forth from conquering to conquer, and to whom battle and victory are synonymous terms, is marching against the doomed city. Jeremiah has all along testified that the only safety is in submission, and counsels his audiences to resist no longer. The war party are very angry at this, and accuse the good man of making the soldiers weak by his words. Eventually, they prevail upon the king to have him cast into the dungeon of Malchiah. "The good old times" must have been hard on men who had to go to prison, if this dungeon was at all typical. It seems to have been more like a very deep cesspool than a cell. Jeremiah was lowered into it, and left there to perish, feeling, doubtless, that he was in a living grave.

Evil was not allowed to have all its own way. There was, at the time we speak of, a native of Africa, who was one of the king's chamberlains, Ebedmelech by name. He, though a man of timid disposition, was very kindly disposed towards the prophet, and having the *entré* to the king, hastened to intercede for the poor prisoner. Zedekiah, who appears to have been about as steadfast as a weathercock, listened to the plea of his servant, and allowed him to have his own way, charging him to take thirty soldiers with him, and save Jeremiah from his fate. This was done without delay, the eunuch taking the precaution to find what might pad the ropes and prevent the flesh of the sufferer being chafed by them, while he was lifted out of the dungeon. For this kind action the prophet was charged with a message to the eunuch, promising him deliverance in the day when the city was carried by storm.

The story is an illustration of the way God saves men. Jeremiah's danger and deliverance were very real. In that dungeon he is, indeed, in "an horrible pit." There was no hope of escape. No light, no firm standing, every prospect of death, and in no long time either. If not eaten by rats, or suffocated, hunger would kill him. Would to God that we preachers could see the real danger to which sinners are exposed! Their evil practices are sure to be their destruction, and it may be under very frightful circumstances. There is a realness about the wages of sin that very few of us feel as we ought, or we should have less lethargy in the pulpit, and more earnestness in our intercourse with those who, because of their unbelief, are under sentence. This world, to many around us, is but a condemned cell, from which there is no escape, until the executioner, Death, pinions his victim, and leads him forth to be destroyed, and that without remedy.

On the other hand, Jeremiah was delivered, brought up out of the miry clay. But the prophet's salvation was only a feeble picture of what God's grace does for those who take hold on Jesus. He remained in the courts of the prison. "Whom the Son makes free are free indeed." We who rest in Jesus may walk about the courts of the King's palace.

> "He breaks the power of cancelled sin,
>   He sets the prisoner free."

In the third chapter of Lamentations we have the prayer of the poor prisoner when in such peril.

> "Mine enemies chased me sore,
>   Like a bird without cause;

They have cut off my life in the dungeon,
And cast a stone upon me;
Waters flowed over my head;
Then I said, I am cut off.
I called upon Thy name, O Lord,
Out of the low dungeon;
Thou hast heard my voice.
Hide not Thine ear at my breathing, at my cry;
Thou drewest near in the day that I called upon
    Thee.
Thou saidst, Fear not!
O Lord, Thou hast pleaded the cause of my soul,
Thou hast redeemed my life."

From this we gather that God revealed Himself in some way, and assured His servant that he should be delivered. Is there some one reading these pages who is afraid of the consequences of his sins? The writer would recommend that he cry earnestly to God. Be not satisfied with some mere form of prayer, but cry aloud to the God of your salvation. He never yet turned back the cry of an earnest soul, and He will assuredly send help from His sanctuary.

Mark you, HELP ALWAYS COMES FROM ABOVE. Jeremiah found it so. It was useless to try to climb out of the dungeon, it was only to fall deeper into the mire. "Salvation is of the Lord." You cannot save yourself. The effort will only exhaust you. Cry unto the Lord. Say, "O Lord, deliver my soul." He is sure to hear your cry. Ebedmelech is only a very poor picture of Jesus. The Saviour does more than send down a rope. He comes Himself and lifts us up. All those of us who are on the way home, are like the sheep that had been lost, and are on the shoulders of the Good Shepherd. Do not be persuaded to doubt the power of Jesus. No pit of sinful habit is too deep for Him. No defilement of sinful pursuits is too filthy for Him to cleanse. He is Omnipotent. "Mighty to save." Saves to the uttermost, whatever that may mean; God's "uttermost" cannot be defined by mortal tongue. "Exceeding abundantly above all that we ask or think." "As the heavens are higher than the earth, so are my ways higher than your ways."

Although Ebedmelech may be a very poor type of Jesus Christ, he is a very good picture of the style in which one man may help another. HE HAD SYMPATHY. The dusky-skinned Ethiopian had a heart that could feel for another. His kind heart bled as he thought of the suffering prophet. Now, sympathy is the mother of help. If some of those who read these pages will look around them, they will see numbers of persons requiring assistance. For instance, see what a crowd of people are in the dungeon of poverty, and many of them deserve it no more than did the prophet. Then there are those who are shut up all their lives in the sick chamber. All the brightness and glory has faded out of their lives. The sun of health has set, and will rise no more! Besides these, there are those who are in the darkened house of bereavement. For them, there seems no hope; they think they have no right to smile: Joy is dead, and must be with the shrouded dead for ever. And do we not know of numbers who are in the dungeon of doubt? Giant Despair keeps on showing them the bones of the prisoners he has slain in bygone days. There are dungeons all around us. Let us have sympathy for them, lest we have to be taught in the same way as Spurgeon tells us Bluff Harry was.

"The story goes, that Harry the Eighth, wandering one night in the streets of London in disguise, was met at the bridge-foot by some of the watch, and not giving a good account of himself, were carried off to the Poultry Compter, and shut up for the night without fire and candle. On his liberation, he made a grant of thirty chaldrons of coals and a quantity of bread for the solace of night prisoners in the Compter. Experience brings sympathy; those who have felt sharp afflictions, terrible convictions, racking doubts, and violent temptations, will be zealous in consoling those in a similar condition. It were well if the great Head of the Church would put unsympathising men, especially ministers, into the Compter of trouble, until they could weep with those that weep."

EBEDMELECH DID NOT ALLOW DIFFICULTY TO DETER HIM. Some men can work hard so long as there are no difficulties ; opposition to them is like a hill on a jibbing horse; they must stop now : they "did not look for this sort of thing, you know." Just so, the eunuch found it was not easy—it never is—to undo wrong. "A stout heart to a stiff brae," is common sense as well as right. "If thou faintest in the day of adversity, thy strength is small." Ebedmelech knew that the enemies of the prophet were unscrupulous, and would not hesitate to cut his throat, but he did not give up because of that. He said, " Ought

Jeremiah to be got out? because, if so, it must be done, whatever may become of me." If you, dear reader, want to have an easy time of it, don't be persuaded to try to do good. Let things drift on without your interference, and you may drift too. It is the easiest way to get along; but we may ride in a first-class carriage to the bottomless pit. If you mean to help others, you will have to pull hard against the stream.

EBEDMELECH TEACHES US TO SPARE THE FEELINGS OF THOSE WE HELP. He lowered down the old rags and clouts he had gathered, and bade the prophet put them under his armpits, so as not to have them cut by the ropes. The rope of deliverance should not cut the flesh of those we save. This is not always thought of. We may wound men in helping them, and they may like the remedy less than the disease. We should think of the feelings, as well as the wants, of those we help. Kind deeds should be expressed in kind words. Some well-intentioned people, in trying to heal one sore, make another, which cannot be healed. We say of some really kind-hearted people, who have very rough words to express kindly ideas, "their bark is worse than their bite;" but why bark at all? It is told of good Bishop Hooper, that once when a penitent went to him in great distress of mind, the bishop looked so stern, and spoke so sharply, that the poor man could not face him, but ran out of the cell where the martyr was imprisoned, and sought some one more kind and gentle. Shall we not imitate Him of whom it is said, "He will not break the bruised reed"? When we take the rope, let us not forget the old rags as well.

Among the practical lessons of this story, there is the great truth that ONE MAN MAY SET OTHERS GOING. Ebedmelech went to the king for help, and he gave him thirty helpers. In the thirteenth verse, we read,

"So *they* drew up Jeremiah." How many times this happens! Robert Raikes had no idea how many wheels his would set in motion. Müller of Bristol has many imitators, and thousands of orphans are fed and clothed that he will never know of. If you will only begin, others will follow you. Don't be afraid of being lonely. Nothing succeeds like success. "To him that hath shall be given." Perhaps, if you don't start, others will not. Not one of those thirty soldiers would have cared to help Jeremiah if Ebedmelech had not. The great mass of people are not original; they can imitate, and if you can show them the way, they will follow. Do not wait for others to start with you; be content to go alone. It was David Livingstone that set Stanley and Cameron to work, and the end of that lonely traveller's work will be seen when "a highway shall be there and the ransomed of the Lord shall return, with songs and everlasting joy upon their heads, and sorrow and sighing shall flee away;" but if Livingstone had waited for others, he would have died, in comfort, it may be, but could not have had a grave in Westminster Abbey, nor have set in motion the plans which are sure to issue in Africa's deliverance.

Let us learn THE VALUE OF DESPISED AND CAST-OFF THINGS. The prudent chamberlain had seen "under the treasury the old cast clouts, and old rotten rags." No one else saw any value in them, but he knew where they lay, and put them to a good use. What a number of men and things are cast aside, like these old rags! Do you see yonder woman in such dismay? What is the matter? She has been upstairs looking at some old dresses of hers, and finds to her horror that the moth has been there before her, and they are useless. Would it not have been better to have given them to her poor relations, or to that widow who has such difficulty to find clothes for her little ones? How happy those children would have been if they could have worn what the moth has eaten! Have you not books you never read which some poor pastor in some country charge could coin into that which would enrich his sermons? Have you not old magazines that would gladden the heart of some of those intelligent paupers who never get any lively reading, or save from *ennui* some convalescent in the hospital? Look and see what you have "under the treasury."

It may be that some of those who read this book feel as though they were useless in the world—men and women who think their chance is gone, and that they are like a cast clout. Very likely the proud nobles of the court thought so of Ebedmelech. He was only "that old nigger," and yet he has lifted himself into the Book of God! Do you think that all the colour has faded out of your life, and your purposes are cut off?

Could you not find some one worse off than yourself, to whom your face would be as that of an angel of God? Could you not nurse the sick, help some weak and weary one, and yet be a comfort to many? Cowper thought himself worse than an old cast clout, and yet his hymns, especially "God moves in a mysterious way," have helped many a tried one to sing in the dark.

Ebedmelech found out that GOD PAYS THE BEST WAGES. He was fearful that in the *melée* he would be slain; but God sent him word, by the mouth of the man he had saved that, "Thou shalt not be given into the hand of the men of whom thou art afraid, but I will deliver thee." This, of all things, was the best news he could hear, and to-day God will pay men in kind, and so we shall sow what we reap. "Light is sown for the righteous."

XIX.

THE LOST AXE.

" The iron did swim."—2 KINGS vi. 6.

THESE words describe something that happened to the servants of God. Iron does not swim for the servants of evil. No such skill has their master, much as he boasts But in how many instances has the "impossible" been accomplished by faith and prayer!

These young men appear to have been divinity students, and the college was too small for them. Elisha's ministry appears to have been blessed much to the young. He had the gravitating power, not merely of greatness, but of great goodness. There is something very interesting about these young men, and especially in the adventure spoken of in this chapter.

THEY WERE INDUSTRIOUS.—Not afraid of hard work. "Take thence every man a beam." This building had to be put up, and they felt they should like to work at it themselves. It is a sorry thing for the ministry when men enter it to be both idle and "respectable." What can be a greater curse than an idle preacher? These young men would not be likely to fall into that snare of the devil, for they liked work. They were something like a young minister the writer has heard of, who, before he went to college, was a coal-miner. He wanted books, so, having some time on his hands during a vacation, he determined to earn some money for books by going down into the mine and hewing coal for a few weeks. It is well for Christians when they have a reputation for being good at work. Why should not our employers say, "I have no one I can trust like that psalm-singer. Ever since he has been what he calls converted, he has been worth twice as much to me as he was before"? The grace of God ought to get into every muscle of our bodies, so that with one eye on heaven, and the other on the earth, we shall be better workmen than ever. These young men took their axes, and every man was to shoulder a beam. Such students would not have shirked either their Greek or mathematics if they had been in our colleges, and the writer feels that he should like to have a colleague from such a set as were willing to toil as these men did.

They were *self-reliant.*—You do not find them going to the prophet whiningly, and saying, "Please, sir, will you call the Committee together, and ask them to get up a subscription towards building us a larger place?" No, they believed in doing it themselves. These men could have told Samuel

Smiles a thing or two in the matter of self-help. They were self-reliant and earnest, believing that God Almighty would bless them if they laid their backs to the work, and were bent on doing their utmost. Could not the Church learn a lesson from the world in this matter? Look for instance at yonder settler in the backwoods. He does not wait for plans. His axe is his architect, and if he marries, he likes to get a woman who is a maid-of-all-work, ready to milk the cow, if she can get one, and do without milk, if her husband cannot afford one, and who can help make a cradle as well as rock it. These are the men and women who are independent of Committees. We want Christians who can show their ministers how to do it, if they don't take the lead themselves. Let us get to work. If you want to be well patronised, patronise yourself.

But though self-reliant, these men were

NOT BUMPTIOUS.—They were not "bad to shoe," as they sometimes say in the north of England. One of the mistakes of self-made men is their bumptiousness; they think no one equal to themselves, and are ready to sneer at all the folk who happen to know who their grandfather was. Not so with these students; they said to the prophet, "I pray thee be content, and go with thy servants." Do you wonder that he said, "I will go"? Old age likes to be thought fit to go with youth. Why does God keep people till they are old? it is that we younger ones should profit by their experience. Let the young man who reads this book never dirty his mouth with the words "Old Fogey." Nor let him be too quick to break home ties, and forget the old folks at home. Your mother *is* your mother, though the light has faded from her eye and the furrows are across her forehead: perhaps anxiety for you put them there.

When you have any new idea, see if you can get old age to go with you to carry your theory into practice. The same thing holds good about books and old-fashioned ideas. The men of to-day have something to learn from the men of the past. Do not too quickly exchange those old puritan folios from your bookshelves for these modern thinkers. And especially is this true of the oldest of books, the Bible; and never begin an enterprise for this world or the next if the Bible does not say with Elisha, "I will go."

These sons of the prophets were HONEST IF POOR.—Poverty cannot always be avoided. It has not been God's way to call only rich men to be his preachers. The plough, the loom, the awl, the fishing-boat keep sending us the men who help to keep the pulpit above mediocrity. And most likely it was so with these students. While one of them was at work with his axe, the head came off, and fell into the muddy stream. He was in trouble about it, and called out, "Alas, master! for it was borrowed." If there had been in that college one of those supremely respectable students who are too refined to shoulder beams, he would not have been so much troubled about the debt, but would have written a polite note to the owner, saying how sorry he was that there should have been such an accident, and hoping that it would not occur again. But he was not there; such men never lose the axe-head: they are not manly enough to take to tree-felling.

It would be well for Christianity if all its professors felt about debt as this man did. It would be well for us if we could not wear clothes that were not paid for. How some of the tradesmen sneer at religion, because they have names that are on the church-roll on the wrong side of their ledgers. It is not honest to order things which cannot be paid for, and it is a kind of Antinomianism that does untold harm for those who call themselves Christians and yet feel no shame for their debts. "Fine feathers make fine birds," but if every young man who has not paid his tailor's bills had to be stripped of his unpaid finery, some would look like unfledged birds. It is well for us, and a sign of grace, when the word "borrowed" calls up a sigh, and "alas!"

Does not this story teach us THE DANGER OF LOOSE THINGS?—The axe-head was loose, and so flew off, and the wonder is that it did not kill somebody. Supposing it had struck the prophet, and slain the man of God? How terrible it would have been; and yet we see old men and women slain every day by the loose habits of their children. Loose habits, like our old clothes, fit us easily, but they are dangerous. Loose company does untold harm,—like some ship in an harbour that has broken from her anchorage, and is dashed against the other ships, doing a great deal of mischief before she sinks. Loose tongues, too, which would be all the better for St. James's bridle. Oh, fasten on the axe-head, lest you do yourself or somebody better a mischief.

What a great deal of TROUBLE IS HOME-MADE. If this man had seen to it that his axe was fast before he began to chop at the tree, the accident would not have happened. Are not many so-called accidents the result of carelessness? Are not men and women slain every day by the want of carefulness? Have we not trouble coming upon us that might have been prevented by common thoughtfulness? Have we not sorrows in our families which we have made ourselves? and home-made trouble, like home-spun linen, wears for many a day. Very likely the man would have said, "I did my best." We have not done our best if we have a loose axe. In the west of Yorkshire, the writer heard a story of an apprentice lad who was chided by his master for something he had done stupidly; the lad whimpered, "I have done my best," and was told, "Ah want noan o' thee best, Ah want thee to do reight." Let us do right, and then we shall put a wedge in all our loose axes.

Have you noticed *how the axe was got up again?*—Iron does not swim without some help. You cannot raise the fallen without an effort. How was it done? "Where fell it? And he shewed him the place. And he cut down a stick, and cast it in thither, and the iron did swim." "EXAMPLE IS BETTER THAN PRECEPT." He did not tell it to swim, he showed it how. We have plenty of preaching the gospel: we want men and women to live it. One of the evils of modern civilization is that large masses of population are left without better example. As soon as men improve their position they go out. Is it any wonder that some parts of London are so rotten? The salt has gone where it is not needed so much. Singing of hymns in some Mission Hall will not attract and tell upon the neighbourhood like the same hymn sung every day at family worship would. If the world is ever raised, it will be by the grace of God acting through the Church upon the sunken masses. Has not God showed us how? Does He call upon us to make a sacrifice He has not done? Jesus did not try to save the world by remaining in heaven. He came down to die,—

> "Down from the shining courts above
> With joyful haste He fled,
> Entered the grave in mortal flesh
> And dwelt among the dead."

What is the cross of Christ but the casting in of the Branch? Yes, this is what has saved us. The cross has "drawn" us up. There is a beautiful little sermon in a verse Charles Wesley used to sing.

It is a sweetly evangelical paraphrase of the story of the lost axe.

> " Deep sunk in nature's base desire,
>   The sinful mud, the worldly mire,
> What but the casting in of grace
>   The fleshly iron heart can raise?
> To heavenly turn my earthly love,
>   And lift my soul to things above!"

XX.

WORN ON THE HEART OF CHRIST.

EXODUS xxxix. 8.

IT is more than likely that when Moses heard the instructions given as to the tabernacle and its splendid furniture, he would be ready to ask, Who is to do the work? The commandment was given before the Divine Being indicated how it was to be done. But whenever God gives the law, He will give the power to obey, and, in this way, commandments become promises. All the time that Moses was wondering, God was preparing. It did seem a real difficulty, the finding of a man of sufficient artistic taste and skill to do all the work that must be done before God could be worshipped according to the ritual He had chosen. Who would have thought of finding, amidst such a horde of slaves as the people of God were, the man needed for the work? and yet he was there.

It may be that this book may fall into the hands of some young man who feels himself very superior to his present circumstances. You want work of a higher order. If you are right in the estimate you have formed of your abilities, God will give you some better work. There is need, pressing need, for men of culture and genius, and if you serve God in the lower place He will call you to higher work in His own time.

In His own time, mark you, for God is in no hurry. We are, and wish to push on the clock of time, but if we do so, it is but for a moment; the hand goes back again. When the time had come for the Church to take hold of India for Christ, there was a man needed for the preparatory work, some one who had the kind of nature which should enable him to plod on for years, grappling with the difficult niceties of the languages, and making the lexicons and dictionaries for other and weaker men to use. And God had the man in training, but did not tell him what He had for him to do. In an obscure village in Northamptonshire, there was a shoemaker, who also was a Baptist preacher. In that man's heart there was a burning desire to go out amongst the heathen. He felt that he had powers which were superior to his position, and that he could spend his time better than in mending shoes, or talking to a handful of rustics who could not appreciate him. One wonders sometimes if there was a sign over his door—

CAREY, BOOT AND SHOE MAKER.

Before he died, he would have needed a much larger one to describe his life work!

Yes, we may settle it, that if Bezaleel will remain in the camp, sooner or later God will give him the carving of gold and engraving of precious stones, and will bring to him Aholiab and others *who " are wise hearted," " to make all that I have commanded."*

Did you ever think of this breastplate, as to its size and shape? In Exodus xxviii. we have a full description of this curiously beautiful ornament. It would seem that what the ladies would call the foundation of it was composed of linen—purple, blue, scarlet—with gold threads, all entwined together. It was made so as to double up when the dress to which it was fastened was taken off. It had four golden rings one at each corner, the two bottom ones being tied to two other rings, which were inserted into the robe called the ephod. The two rings at the top corners were fastened to two golden chains, and the chains looped up to the two precious stones which fitted like epaulettes on the shoulders of the high priest. But the most splendid parts of this ornament were the twelve precious stones, which were placed in four rows, and on each of which was graven the name of one of the tribes, so that each of the tribes was borne on the breast of the high priest.

What a picture of Jesus Christ, as He is in His glory! Aaron with the breastplate is a type of Jesus, carrying the Church of God on his heart. No type can teach all the truth respecting Jesus, for Aaron did not always wear the breastplate. He often took it off. Not so with our High Priest, who has entered into the heavens.

If you will take the pains to look into the book of Exodus, you will find that there is a very full description of this ornament, and it is given twice over. It is evident that we are to expect some lessons of practical use to the Church in all ages, and if we will look at this breastplate as a picture of the Church, we may learn what may be of use to us in the present day.

There were TWELVE stones, each of them different, and each bearing a different name. Not one stone, with a solitary name. WHAT VARIETY! Shall we ever get one comprehensive community from which there can be no dissent? That has been the dream of many an enthusiast, and the hope of its accomplishment has made gentle hearts able to tolerate the idea of persecuting those who differ from them. So long as the human race differs so much in mental structure, we shall not be able to think alike, even in those things which are spoken of in Holy Writ. *Baptism*, for instance; most Christian men are agreed that it is obligatory: but what a difference of opinion. One would baptize every child; another, none but the children of believers, while another cannot see why you should sprinkle infants; he would have none but adults, or at least believers, and these should be immersed; while the so-called Quaker believes that water is not needed at all. To him, baptism is altogether a spiritual thing.

What differences with regard to worship! Some must have a form; and who can deny that many who use the book of Common Prayer do so in the most devout spirit, and not in vain, as their holy lives declare, for their Father who seeth in secret rewards them openly? Others are shocked at the idea of calling such worship prayer. They can find no prayers like those which well up from their own heart. They cannot use any one else's words; and you feel they are right, so far as their own experience goes. One man is not at home worshipping anywhere, but in some venerable building, with its long sweep of Gothic aisles, and never is lifted so near to the angels as when the paid surpliced choir is singing, "We praise

WORN ON THE HEART OF CHRIST. 241

Thee, O God," while another, equally faithful, is aghast at the thought of any one being paid for praising the Lord!

What difference in religious feeling and experience! We find some joyous, and filled with holy enthusiasm, while others are pensive and almost melancholy. Here is one who likes to sing Charles Wesley's joyous strains, while another is most at home reading in secret Keble's "Christian Year." Some tremble for the ark of God; others shout the battle-cry, and laugh at the thought of defeat. We are not alike. We are opposites of each other, and yet differ only as the stones on the breastplate; one is blue, another yellow, here is a bright ruby, there a sparkling emerald, while another is the colourless yet splendid diamond! But all on the same breastplate.

This brings us to another truth,—THE UNITY OF THE CHURCH. All differing, yet all on the heart of Christ. Some of the stones were in the same row, though differing in colour; others were as far apart as possible, yet each on the heart of the high priest. It is well for us to learn that each lover of God is as near to His heart as any other of His dear ones. There are great contrasts in style and expression, both of doctrine and ritual, perhaps never more so than to-day, yet we are nearer together than we think for. The High Churchman, who loves God worshipping in his beautiful Cathedral, with its stained glass and pealing anthems, seems to be a long way from "the Brethren" who, in some humble upper room, try to reproduce the simple breaking of bread; and yet they are but at the opposite corners of the breastplate, for they agree in loving and reverencing the Christ of God. Charles Haddon Spurgeon and Canon Liddon differ vastly in many things, but it would be hard to say which of them is the most vehement in his hatred of sin, and the most courageous in denouncing the vile thing that dishonours God.

No one can mix much in the Churches of Christ without perceiving, amidst all the contrasts, the strong love there is for the Master. There is unity in this, any way, and this is the most important. If we had persecutions as our heritage, there is not one of the different sects but would furnish its quota of men and women who would go down to death singing in triumph. Doubtless, before to-day, there have been burned at the same stake men who differed in some minor doctrine or ritual.

We get an illustration of the unity of the Church when some enemy of God writes a book which threatens to destroy the foundations of faith. There and then, men who differ much, yet agree in this, to sit down and write some vigorous answer to the common foe. The Temperance platform is to-day what the Anti-Slavery platform used to be,—a sort of breastplate, on which men may be found, wide apart in all but love for God and hatred to sin.

Melancthon used to tell a story when any sneered or sorrowed about the divisions in the Church. "We are not so far apart as you think," he would say. "Did you ever hear of the time when the shepherds' dogs quarrelled and fought? The wolves heard of it, and thought that the time had come for them to go down and take the sheep. However, one wiser than the rest suggested that one of their number should go first, and see how matters stood. He came back sooner than was expected, and was asked. Are the dogs quarrelling? Yes. Well, shall we go? No, said he, for though I heard them snarling and snapping as I came down the hill, as soon as they saw me they gave up fighting, and came at me, so that I had hard work to escape!"

So it is to-day. The enemy has only to

show himself, and men who differ amongst themselves agree to drive him back. The pity is that they do not see the need there is, not only for the love of God, but the love of the brother also. Let us learn from the different precious stones being on the same breastplate not to be vexed at the others for not being the same colour as ourselves, but thankful that He accepts us as well as them; and let us show our gratitude by shining and sparkling as much as possible.

They were all precious stones; not one was mean or contemptible. God's Church has ever been COSTLY. No jewel is what it afterwards becomes when first found. Diamonds, before they have been in the hands of the lapidary, seem of little beauty. But they pay for the pains they cost. What would poor human nature be but for what God has spent upon it? If it were not for the love of God in Jesus Christ, we should wonder that He should be so patient with us, and that he bears with us in our education and training. Yet when we think of Gethsemane and Calvary, we can understand all the rest. If God can so love us when we are sinners, no wonder that He loves us when we repent and believe on Jesus.

Shall not those of us who have been long in the Church of God bear with the ignorance and folly of those who have only just been dug out of the mine? Let not the stone which sparkles in its setting sneer at that which only looks like a pebble. The Master has chosen it; He knows that He has put within its rude exterior that which only needs time and skill to make it "shine as the stars for ever and ever."

"Beloved, if God so loved us, we ought also to love one another." If God has chosen us, who would yet have been pebbles but for His grace that picked us up, and worked out His design in us, shall we not love the rest of His Church? Other Christians are of value to God; the most lowly-born and ignorant of His saints cost God as much as the most wealthy or refined. Shall we not feel rather ashamed when we get to heaven, and see there some whom we would not speak to on earth? As we come in at the North Gate, others will enter from the South. We shall "sit down" with them in our Father's house above: why should we not sit down together in our houses below? Pure religion is to visit the fatherless and widows in their affliction; we shall be glad enough to visit some of these in their mansions of glory: should we not visit them now in their cellars and garrets?

If God sets such a value upon us, shall we not set value upon ourselves. Not in the way of pride or vainglory, but in the abhorrence of evil, and even in avoiding the appearance of it. God having loved us and set us apart for Himself, "let us cleanse ourselves from all filthiness of the flesh and spirit, perfecting holiness in the fear of God."

Why were these precious stones put upon the breastplate? They were not on the mitre; no, they were upon the heart, teaching us that the Church is BELOVED. We need not then to envy John, that he was allowed to lean on the breast of Jesus. Is not every believer there? If we do not hear the beating of Christ's heart, it is because we do not listen for it. One reason why we allow ourselves to be brought into heaviness is because we lose sight of the fact that God is loving us as much now as when He punished His Son for our sins. The love of God is like everything else of His, not changeable. You are loving One who appreciates your affection, and who will not waste your heart's love. Oh, how much love is thrown away! Men and women pouring out their heart's chief treasure on those who are altogether unworthy of it. If we loved

God with the same intensity that we often love our fellows, how He would delight Himself in us! Have you, in your readings in the Prophets, marked how the Divine Being bewails the love which His chosen people have wasted upon unworthy objects? how He yearns to have back the love they once showed to Him? And He is the same to-day; there is a mine of spiritual meaning in the words, "I love them that love me." And is there any way of learning to love God like knowing His love to us? Think then of the place you hold in God's affection. You are on the heart of the High Priest. You may have been under some misapprehension on this point, and have grieved over what seemed His forgetfulness of you.

Do you see yonder woman, who is bidding good-bye to her son? He is leaving the quiet farm-house where he was born, and going up to London to a situation. His mother has given him, as a parting present, a locket with her likeness, for which he kisses her. He promises to write every week, and so they part. A few months roll past, and every week comes the looked-for letter. But one morning, the letter day, there is no tidings, and the next, and the next! Oh, dear, what is the matter? Can he have forgotten me? A few days more, and there comes a telegram from his lodgings, telling that the lad is very ill, and seems likely to die. How soon the mother is gone! She arrives at the lodgings. Thank God the blinds are not down! She is shown into his room. He is insensible. Does not know her; but lies quiet, and yet is in the grasp of fierce disease. She sits awhile, and then, mother-like, looks at his books and papers, folds up his clothes. There is his watch and pocket-book, but she does not see the locket. It will be in some of his pockets. She looks: no; well, but in his desk, hid away under his papers? No; can he have lost it?

How jealous she is as she finds cartes-de-visite of friends and companions, but no locket. She cannot ask him, for he knows nothing. Ah me, my boy has forgotten his mother, and has lost the likeness he once kissed so fondly. But now he turns over, and the anxious mother hastens to shake his pillow, when, see, there is something bright under his shirt,—yes, next his heart is the locket, and he is more precious than ever!

Believer, thou art on the breast of God!

We cannot read with attention the description given of this type of the Church without noticing the great pains which were taken to keep it from being lost. It was not only fastened to the shoulders by chains, themselves as strong as they were beautiful, but the bottom part of the breastplate was fastened by two rings lashed to the two rings which were put into the ephod for the purpose of holding the ornament. Does not this tell us of the SECURITY of the Church? As we think of these chains and lashings, how can we help thinking of one who said, "Who shall separate us from the love of Christ?" You fear, dear reader, sometimes, that you shall not be able to hold out to the end. Think again: it is not you, but God. "Perfect love casteth out fear." Not merely your love, which in some sense can never be perfect, but the love of God, which is perfection. We wonder what became of the breastplate. Did it survive all the changes in Jewish history? We do not read of any other being made. Is it in existence to-day? Precious stones are not like metals that could be melted down and made into some other ornaments. So far as we know, not one of these stones has been destroyed. Did Titus carry the precious thing to Rome, and has it been thrown into the Tiber? Or is it among the stores of wealth in jewels possessed by the Turk?

Constantinople has some rare and wondrous jewels; has it the twelve? We know not; but we do know that Christ has said, "No man shall pluck them out of my hand." "They shall be mine, saith the Lord of Hosts, in that day when I make up my jewels." Still there is the thief; Jesus tells us that he cometh to steal! Watch therefore! It is most instructive that in the same discourse Jesus speaks both of the thief coming to steal, and the security of those who hear His voice and follow Him.

The writer knew an aged disciple who was wont to tell how, fifty years before, she had been brought to Christ, and made very happy in His love. Several other young people had at the same time been much impressed, and for a time bade fair to reach the kingdom, but 'twas but for a season. To her great surprise and grief, they went back again. She was warned by the defection of her companions, and at times filled with fear that she should "also go away." So much did she feel it that one night, as she was walking home over the fields, just as she was crossing a dyke by a narrow foot bridge, she kneeled down on the plank, and clinging to the rail, cried mightily to the Lord that He would keep her to the end; and so, fifty years after, she could rejoice in the prospect of death. The golden chains kept the breastplate in its place.

> " My soul into Thy hands I give,
> And if he can obtain Thy leave,
> Let Satan pluck me thence."

XXI.

THE BATTLE OF MICHMASH.

1 SAMUEL xiv.

THESE were evil days for the people of Israel. Their enemies, the Philistines, had so subdued them that it was a crime to possess a weapon of any kind. Nor was there a smith to be found. If the farmer's ploughshare wanted sharpening, he had to take it to the Philistines. But it was in these dark days that Jonathan shone so famous. It is yet true that difficulties prove our mettle, and that the greater the hardship or peril, the more is the victory worth telling. Poets do not sing, though newspapers may print, the account of some brilliant review; but let "the six hundred" obey, and snatch honour from the teeth of hell, and Tennyson makes the deed immortal. The Philistines were encamped on the brow of a cliff, and were in a position which they fondly thought was impregnable; but the brave son of Saul felt that he could not bear to see the foe of his country, like some eagle on a lofty crag, from which it could with ease descend to prey upon the flocks.

THE PRESENCE OF THE ENEMY SHOULD ROUSE OUR COURAGE. Jonathan could not allow the Philistines to be even at Michmash, strong as it was, without striking a blow. "What!" said he, "shall these enemies of my country continue to oppress us, and we submit to their tyranny? It is true they are very strong, but I cannot bear to see them where they are, and not fight." Is there not need for more chivalry among the soldiers of Christ? How sin lords it over us, even in England. Intemperance, lust, cruelty, ignorance, are the enemies of our land; and they do almost as they like; they are slaying our people, starving our children, dishonouring our women. Think, for instance, of the history of one gin-palace. If we could have the details of one year's crime and sorrow produced by one such place, it would freeze our heart's blood. Did the inhabitants of any foreign country do us the same wrong, our nation would be in a blaze; armies would be levied, the senate would vote us money, and very soon that nation would have to sue for mercy or fight for life.

Where are our Jonathans? How can they allow the Philistines to enslave us, and to slay our children, without making greater efforts? If we could not tolerate the presence of an invading foe, if it would drive us to madness to see the royal standard of some other country wave over Windsor Castle, how can we bear to see the arrogance and cruelty of the enemies of Jesus Christ in this so-called Christian land?

It was Jonathan who conceived the plan of attacking the Philistines; which leads us to say—PRINCES SHOULD SET THE EXAMPLE. It was not the armour-bearer who was the first to speak. Jonathan said: "Come, and let us go over unto the garrison of these uncircumcised." If God has lifted you, my reader, out of the ranks, demean yourself accordingly. Officers, to the front. It is a shame when a private has to lead a forlorn hope; and yet too often in Church history we find the poor and the ignorant more full of zeal for God than the rich and learned. Have you wealth?—use it as becomes a prince of God. Are there not numbers of men who would be ready to fight for God if they could be sustained? You have the means: use them for God and righteousness. Have you learning?—use it to slay ignorance. Could you not teach some of those who are willing to fight, but do not know the use of weapons? Have you the gift of utterance? Has God endowed you with the kingliness of speech? Then why be dumb, when your voice ought to be ringing out for the right and the true!

Why do not our Jonathans lead us forth? Why do they leave the conduct of the army to those whom we cannot respect as we should a prince? Set the key-note. "Lift up your voice with strength." There are thousands who, like the armour-bearer, only want someone to say, "Come, and let us go over," and they would spring upon the foe with irresistible force. How the example of Lord Shaftesbury has animated weaker men, and made them feel like the armour-bearer of Jonathan.

It is true that EARNEST LEADERS SHOULD NOT LACK BRAVE FOLLOWERS. We are not told the name of the young man who was Jonathan's armour-bearer, but he was worthy of the situation. Listen to him: *"Do all that is in thine heart: turn thee; behold, I am with thee according to thy heart."* As if he had said, "Look at me: do I look like flinching? If thou art first, I will be second! I am ready to follow thy lead: thou canst not go where I will not be close behind." If Jesus Christ could only have a Church like that armour-bearer, how soon the victory would be ours! How many earnest ministers there are whose hearts ache with vexation because their efforts are not seconded by their people! In how many cases the superintendent of the Sunday-school is sorely tried by the want of punctual and painstaking teachers! Do we not know men who are willing to preach in the open air, and yet they must do it alone,—no one to help them to sing, or to stand by them. Should this be so?

How pleased Jonathan must have been with the answer of his armour-bearer! How much easier it was to climb the steep hill, and to face the Philistines, as he thought of the brave man who was following. And it is yet true that the best of leaders is all the better for the knowledge that his followers will not fail him. Let those of us whose place is not to lead, yet help our commander by acting, so that whenever he looks at us he will see our faces say, " I am with thee according to thy heart."

Jonathan knew that GOD CAN WIN BY A MINORITY. He said to his companion, "*There is no restraint to the Lord to save by many or by few.*" He remembered that God had promised, "One shall chase a thousand, two put ten thousand to flight." If, in fighting the Lord's battles, we wait till we outnumber the foe, we shall never "do exploits." Joshua and Caleb were outvoted, but they said, "Let us go up at once and possess it." The twelve apostles did not wait, but, in the teeth of the Sanhedrim, preached "Jesus and the resurrection." The Reformers were in a minority, but they made the world ring with their protests against priestly arrogance and superstition. At one time John Wesley was almost the only clergyman who dared the rotten eggs of the Philistines of his day, and now he and his brother have a monument in Westminster Abbey!

If you, dear reader, feel that God has called you to do work for Him, begin at once. Do not wait till you have an army at your back: they may only hinder you. Make a beginning, and remember that in the work of God "there is no restraint to the Lord." The fewer there are, the more room for Omnipotence. The units of Christian workers are the thin end of the wedge. Some one must go first. Why should it not be you?

At the battle of Michmash, we have been taught that GOD HELPS THEM WHO HELP THEMSELVES. Jonathan said to his companion, "When we show ourselves, if they say, 'Come up,' we shall know the Lord means us to win." So they climbed up on their hands and knees, and after a while, the soldiers saw them, and sneeringly said, "The Hebrews come forth out of the holes." They then cried out, "Come up to us, and we will show you a thing." How Jonathan would smile as he thought, "The Lord has delivered them into our hand." Very soon he and the armour-bearer were at the top, and the fight began. There were about twenty men killed, and then came an earthquake;—God worked with the brave men who had gone alone. This "trembling of God," as it is called in the margin, struck a panic into the hearts of the Philistines. So much so that the Philistines lost their senses, and began to fight one another, and when Saul arrived on the scene he saw that "every man's sword was against his fellow."

This might have happened if Jonathan had not gone up, but most likely not. God works yet by means, and delights in co-operating with His people. If you want God to help you, help yourself. Climb up the hill in spite of Philistinic sneers, and when you are at the top, the earth shall quake. You will not be alone very long. Saul brought his army after the brave pair had gone alone, and the number of Saul's people increased directly, as you read in verses 21, 22. The enslaved Hebrews rose against their masters, and these also who had hid themselves, "*when they heard that the Philistines fled, even they also followed hard after them in the battle.*" This is not said to their honour. Do not wait, then till the enemy has fled, but turn the battle by your bravery, even if it be by a single hand. But let us give God the glory of His grace. Whether we win by ones or by thousands, let us sing, as we shall in those glorious days when the enemy flees only to fall into the bottomless pit, and write it on the banner of the host,

"SO THE LORD SAVED ISRAEL THAT DAY."

27, PATERNOSTER ROW, LONDON.

HODDER AND STOUGHTON'S
PUBLICATIONS.

BROWNLOW NORTH;
RECORDS AND RECOLLECTIONS.
BY THE REV.
KENNETH MOODY STUART, M.A.

Crown 8vo, cloth, price 7s. 6d.

This Memorial volume of this well-known Evangelist consists of a biographical sketch of his earlier years, a narrative of his evangelistic labours, and a review of the substance and character of his preaching. The titles of the chapters are:—

- I. Brownlow North's Earlier Years.
- II. Brownlow North's Conversion.
- III. First Private Efforts to Win Souls.
- IV. Early Evangelistic Work.
- V. Lay Preaching.
- VI. His Recognition as an Evangelist by the Free Church of Scotland.
- VII. Brownlow North's Post-bag.
- VIII. Brownlow North's Portfolio.
- IX. AND X. Brownlow North's Theology; comprising:—
    - (1) Existence and Personality of God.
    - (2) Inspiration of Scripture.
    - (3) Immortality of the Soul.
    - (4) The New Birth.
    - (5) Justification by Faith not Feeling.
- XI. Work in Ireland and in London.
- XII. Harvest Work in various Fields.
- XIII. Remarkable Cases of Conversion.
- XIV. AND XV. Extracts from his Annotated Bibles, Addresses, etc.
- XVI. Later Evangelistic Labours.
- XVII. Last Year of Labour in Glasgow.
- XVIII. Reminiscences by Personal Friends.
- XIX. Entrance into Rest.

Hodder and Stoughton,

Crown 8vo, cloth, price 3s. 6d.

OUR BLUE JACKETS.
A NARRATIVE OF MISS WESTON'S LIFE AND WORK AMONG OUR SAILORS.
BY AN EYE-WITNESS.
With three Full-Page Illustrations.

CONTENTS :—

Early Life—Small Beginnings—Monthly Letters, or "Blue Backs"—Temperance Work—Story of the Purchase and Fitting up of the Sailors' Rest and Institute—First Years' Work at the Sailors' Rest—Future Prospects—Appendix—"How I spent Three Days at the Sailors' Rest."

Eleventh Thousand, Fcap. 8vo, cloth, 1s. 6d.

HEART LIFE.
BY REV. DR. CUYLER.

"None of the religious literature of the day is fresher, healthier, or more spiritual. We return to their short chapters with unwearied zest, and always find them literally *heart life.*"—*Christian.*

"A series of brief, pointed, and practical papers, and we cannot wonder that Dr. Cuyler's simple, straightforward, and penetrating words have found a large audience."—*Christian World.*

Eighth Thousand, Fcap. 8vo, cloth, 1s. 6d.

HEART THOUGHTS.
BY REV. DR. CUYLER.

"The freshness of thought and the choice words he uses give a charm to what he has written. They are most enjoyable reading." — *Weekly Review.*

"These books have already abundantly justified their existence. They consist of short, stirring sermonettes, and are well adapted for gift books."—*Baptist.*

Third Edition, Fcap. 8vo, cloth, 3s. 6d.

THOUGHTS FOR HEART AND LIFE,

Being "Heart Life," "Heart Thoughts," and "Heart Culture," bound in one volume.

"Just the book to take up in spare minutes. The thoughtful and vigorous tone maintained throughout is most welcome."—*Rock.*

"This book, with its fresh and stimulating thoughts, is worthy of being in every home."—*Evangelical Magazine.*

Hodder and Stoughton,

Crown 8vo, cloth, price 3s. 6d.

POINTED PAPERS

FOR THE CHRISTIAN LIFE,

BY THEODORE L. CUYLER, D.D.

"A series of practical papers on the Christian life,—from the soul's first step towards Jesus Christ, clear onward to its final home-coming into heaven."—*From Preface.*

CONTENTS :—

Not Far Off.
Two kinds of Inquirers.
Build for Eternity !
Take up thy Bed and Walk.
The Returning Dove.
One Honest Hour with Jesus.
The Conversion at the Toll-booth.
Christ, and His Little Ships.
Follow thou Me !
Jesus the Light-Giver.
Jesus the Joy-Bringer.
The Silver Spring, and its Lessons.
After Conversion : What Next ?
Teaching Beginners how to Walk.
What are you a Christian for ?
Wholly for Christ.
The Christian the World's Bible.
"Master ! "
Cautions to Christians.
The Stone that stops the Blessing.
What every Backslider needs.
The Great Seven-fold Prayer.
Christ as the Soul's Trustee.
How well Jesus knows Us.
Seven Things we know about Jesus.

Held by the Right Hand.
" So did not I."
Rooted by the Rivers.
Help from the Throne.
The Secret of Power.
Life more Abundantly.
The Soul's Eagle-flight.
God's Singers.
A Golden Motto for every Christian.
The Hands of Christ.
Ups and Downs.
Fear not ; Only Trust !
The Everlasting Arms.
A Lift for the Overloaded.
God's Kindness to the Crippled.
Four Anchors.
Rest for the Restless.
Refining the Gold.
Time and Place for meeting Jesus.
The Face towards Jerusalem.
Nearer to God.
Treasures in Heaven.
Light at Evening-Time.
Knowing our Friends in Heaven.

27, Paternoster Row.

8vo, cloth, price 12s.
THE BAMPTON LECTURES FOR 1878.

ZECHARIAH AND HIS PROPHECIES.

ESPECIALLY THE MESSIANIC, CONSIDERED IN RELATION TO MODERN CRITICISM.

With a Critically-Revised Translation of the Original Hebrew, and a Critical and Grammatical Commentary on the Entire Book.

BY THE REV. C. H. H. WRIGHT, B.D., M.A., Ph.D,
Incumbent of St. Mary's, Belfast.

Large 4to, cloth, price 18s.

THE
Englishman's Critical and Expository
BIBLE CYCLOPÆDIA.

Compiled and Written

BY THE REV. A. R. FAUSSET, A.M.,
Joint Author of the "Critical and Experimental Commentary."

WITH MORE THAN SIX HUNDRED ILLUSTRATIVE WOODCUTS.

The aim of this work is to place within the reach of all the fruits of modern criticism and research, and at the same time to set forth, briefly and suggestively, those doctrinal and experimental truths which the Written Word itself contains. The labours of the agents of the Palestine Exploration Fund have thrown fresh light on many obscure questions of sacred topography and history. The discoveries thus made, in so far as they elucidate the sacred volume, have been embodied in this Cyclopædia. Many subjects which some of the Bible Dictionaries omit, and which are of deep interest, are included. It is a storehouse of Scriptural information in a most compact and accessible form; and at the end is an index of all the books and almost all the chapters in the Bible, in consecutive order, with references to the articles which illustrate them.

27, *Paternoster Row.*

BY THE REV. L. TYERMAN.

In two volumes, 8vo, 24s. with Portraits.

THE LIFE OF THE REV. GEORGE WHITEFIELD, B.A.

"Mr. Tyerman has conferred a benefit on the whole Methodist world by his 'Life of George Whitefield.' There is as general a desire to know more about the great Methodist orator as to know more about the founder of Methodism. Having supplied one of these wants by his excellent Life of Wesley, Mr. Tyerman has now, in a style equal if not superior to his other great work, supplied the other. He has presented, in a most graphic manner, a living picture before us, and we close his volumes with regret. Every Methodist should have in his library this Life as companion to the 'Life and Times of the Rev. John Wesley,' by the same accomplished and painstaking writer." — *Methodist Recorder.*

8vo, cloth, with Portraits, price 7s. 6d. each Volume.

THE LIFE AND TIMES OF THE REV. JOHN WESLEY, M.A.

CHEAPER EDITION.

"It deserves the praise, not only of being the fullest biography of Wesley, but also of being eminently painstaking, veracious, and trustworthy."—*Edinburgh Review.*

"The narratives of travel through England, Scotland, and Ireland, the records of evangelistic labour, the gradual building up of Wesleyanism as a system, form a history of great interest, and allure the reader on from chapter to chapter with all the attraction of a romance. We cannot doubt that Mr. Tyerman's work, so rich and abundant in materials, will henceforth be regarded as the standard life of Wesley."—*The Evangelical Magazine.*

8vo., cloth, price 10s. 6d. with Portraits.

THE OXFORD METHODISTS:
MEMOIRS OF CLAYTON, INGHAM, GAMBOLD, HERVEY, AND BROUGHTON, ETC.,

"Readers of Mr. Tyerman's previous volumes will be especially thankful for this companion. It is distinguished by all the excellences of its predecessors, and completes a very valuable contribution to the history of the last century."—*British Quarterly Review.*

Hodder and Stoughton,

Seventh Edition, fcap. 8vo, price 3s. 6d.

TALKING TO THE CHILDREN.

BY ALEXANDER MACLEOD, D.D.

"An exquisite work. Divine truths are here presented in simple language, illustrated by parable and anecdote at once apt and beautiful."—*Evangelical Magazine.*

"Simple and interesting, and yet orderly and rich in Gospel truth. The book is full of illustrative matter, used most adroitly and pertinently."—*Sunday School Chronicle.*

Third Thousand, crown 8vo, cloth, 3s. 6d.

GLIMPSES OF THE INNER LIFE OF OUR LORD.

BY PROFESSOR W. G. BLAIKIE, D.D., LL.D.

"Dr. Blaikie divides his book into twelve lectures, in each of which a special phase of Christ's inner life is presented for consideration and imitation. Many valuable and beautiful passages there are in the course of the book."—*Nonconformist.*

"A devout, spiritual, and tender little book, reverently seeking to penetrate the religious heart of Jesus in His consecration, temptations, ministering, sorrows, prayerfulness, peace, joy, cross-bearing, and death."—*British Quarterly Review.*

Second and Cheap Edition, fcap. 8vo, cloth, price 2s. 6d.

THE GLORY OF THE CROSS,

AS MANIFESTED BY THE LAST WORDS OF JESUS.

BY A. B. MACKAY.

"A choice theme, handled with much reverence and spiritual power."—*C. H. Spurgeon, in the "Sword and Trowel."*

"This is a good volume. With careful pains the author shows us the successive scenes of the crucifixion, and teaches us their meanings. He makes his instructions vivid and bright with well-chosen epithet and illustration, and presses the conscience with energy to receive the gospel of love."—*Dr. Dykes, in the "British and Foreign Evangelical Review."*

Second Edition, crown 8vo, cloth, price 5s.

THE FULNESS OF BLESSING;

OR,

THE GOSPEL OF CHRIST AS ILLUSTRATED FROM THE BOOK OF JOSHUA.

BY SARAH F. SMILEY.

"We deem this an esoteric explanation of the Book of Joshua of a very high order. If we view it as Miss Smiley has so carefully done, we shall have before us, as is well said, 'a picture the grandest in its proportions, the most lifelike in its groupings, the most striking in its wealth of colouring, and the most skilful in its quiet touches, of any that God has given us in this royal art-gallery of truth.'"—*Record.*

Crown 8vo, price 5s.

CHRISTIAN SUNSETS;

OR,

THE LAST HOURS OF BELIEVERS.

BY THE REV. JAMES FLEMING, D.D.,
Author of "Remarkable Conversions."

"A very welcome volume. Dr. Fleming tells the facts he has to record in simple, earnest, impressive words. The result is—a most instructive little volume, showing how Christians die."—*Freeman.*

"He shows clearly enough that the hour of death is illuminated and gladdened by the conscious presence of Him who has brought life and immortality to light by the Gospel.—*Christian World.*

Crown 8vo, cloth, elegant, 7s. 6d. Gilt edges, 8s.

SACRED STREAMS.

THE ANCIENT AND MODERN HISTORY OF THE RIVERS OF THE BIBLE.

BY PHILIP HENRY GOSSE, F.R.S.

With forty-four Illustrations, and a Map. A New Edition, revised by the Author.

"Here is a great treat for the Christian reader. Those who know how Mr. Gosse blends the naturalist and the earnest believer will form a shrewd idea of how he treats his subject and makes the Rivers of the Bible stream with instruction."—*Rev. C. H. Spurgeon in "Sword and Trowel."*

Hodder and Stoughton,

Volume I., Matthew and Mark. Crown 8vo, cloth, price 5s.

A POPULAR COMMENTARY ON THE NEW TESTAMENT.

Comprising the Text, with Marginal References, Copious Explanatory Notes, and Numerous Maps, Plans, and Engravings.

BY D. D. WHEDON, D.D., LL.D.

"This is a very sensible commentary, replete with sound information. Dr. Whedon has made the reader of his commentary aware of all the light which modern travel and geographical research have thrown on the evangelic history."—*British Quarterly Review.*

Volume II., Luke and John. Crown 8vo, cloth, price 5s.

A POPULAR COMMENTARY ON THE NEW TESTAMENT.

"Thoughtful scholarship and evangelical simplicity combine to give a charm to this commentary, which will commend it alike to the student and the devotional reader. Really good illustrations add to the attractiveness of the volumes."—*The Fireside.*

Volume III., Acts and Romans. Crown 8vo, cloth, price 5s.

A POPULAR COMMENTARY ON THE NEW TESTAMENT.

"It is carefully written; and the author is conversant with the works of many previous expositors. His comments are for the most part brief, compressed, and to the purpose."—*Expositor.*

Volume IV., 1 Cor. to 2 Timothy. Crown 8vo, cloth, price 5s.

A POPULAR COMMENTARY ON THE NEW TESTAMENT.

"The illustrations, plans, and maps are numerous and well executed. Dr. Whedon writes with singular independence of view and much happiness of expression. We know of no commentary with so good and so valuable a fund of information within so small a space."—*Standard.*

Volume V., completing the work, will be published in 1879.

H. K. WOOD.

I.

THE HEAVENLY BRIDEGROOM AND HIS BRIDE.

BY H. K. WOOD.

Crown 8vo, cloth, price 3s. 6d.

"The Heavenly Bridegroom and His Bride are, we doubt not, figuratively delineated in 'The Song of Songs, which is Solomon's.' Holding it to be truly an allegory, and, as an old puritan minister once said, 'a book of fondness between Christ and His people,' the author has endeavoured to open up briefly its spiritual teachings, and to illustrate them, in a popular style, with a considerable variety of anecdotal and biographical matter, much of it original. Throughout, his aim has been to attract sinners to the Saviour, and to encourage believers."—*From the Preface.*

II.

THE HIGHWAY OF SALVATION.

Sixth Thousand, fcap. 8vo, cloth, 1s. 6d.

"Of this emphatically 'good book' it may be truly said, that the farther its reader advances, the more will he enjoy its perusal. An admirable and excellent little work. For 'The Highway of Salvation' a wide and general circulation is greatly to be desired."—*Record.*

III.

HEAVENLY LOVE AND EARTHLY ECHOES.

Sixteenth Thousand, fcap. 8vo, cloth, 1s. 6d.

"The treatment is most appropriate, winning, and earnest. The various joys and sorrows of life, the vicissitudes, fears, hopes, and victories of Christian experience, furnish many fascinating and impressive illustrations of the Father's love. The book is an admirable specimen of 'experimental' Christian teaching."—*General Baptist Magazine.*

REV. WILLIAM JAY'S WORKS.

In Eight Handsome Volumes, each Volume being complete in itself and sold separately. Crown 8vo, Roxburghe Binding. Price 5s. each. An entirely New Re-Issue, comprising—

    I. **Morning and Evening Exercises.**
        JANUARY TO MARCH.
   II. **Morning and Evening Exercises.**
        APRIL TO JUNE.
  III. **Morning and Evening Exercises.**
        JULY TO SEPTEMBER.
  IV. **Morning and Evening Exercises.**
        OCTOBER TO DECEMBER.
   V. **Family Prayers for Six Weeks, Morning and Evening.**
        Printed in Large Type.
  VI. **Short Discourses.**
        To be read in Families. Volume I.
 VII. **Short Discourses.**
        To be read in Families. Volume II.
VIII. **The Christian Contemplated.**

Fifth Thousand, fcap. 8vo, cloth, 2s. 6d.

A YOUNG MAN'S DIFFICULTIES WITH HIS BIBLE.

BY THE REV. D. W. FAUNCE, D.D.,
Author of "The Christian in the World."

"Clear, able, considerate, and condenses a large amount of argument on the questions that are being asked at the present time."—*Christian World.*

"As far as we can see, no real difficulty is omitted, and there is evidence of considerable research and ability."—*Church Sunday School Magazine.*

Second Thousand, fcap. 8vo, cloth, 2s. 6d.

A YOUNG MAN'S SAFEGUARD IN THE PERILS OF THE AGE.

BY THE REV. W. GUEST, F.G.S.,
Author of "Fidelia Fiske," etc.

"A book of invaluable counsel, and as brave and masculine in its tone as it is tender and yearning in its sympathy. It is from a mind well stored and from a heart brimful of love."—*Methodist Recorder.*

"We have read this book with unabated interest. There is a manly Christian tone throughout, which cannot fail to arrest the attention and win the confidence of the reader."—*Young Men's Christian Magazine.*

27, Paternoster Row.

Monthly, price One Shilling.

THE EXPOSITOR.

EDITED BY THE REV. SAMUEL COX.

The First Seven Volumes are now ready, handsomely bound in cloth, 8vo, price 7s. 6d. each.

Cases for Binding Numbers in Half-Yearly Volumes, 1s. each.

WORKS BY THE EDITOR OF "THE EXPOSITOR."

I.

EXPOSITORY ESSAYS AND DISCOURSES.

Crown 8vo, cloth, price 8s. 6d.

"A new series of EXPOSITORY ESSAYS AND DISCOURSES, by Samuel Cox, deserves the most cordial welcome we can accord it. A more helpful book for students and ministers it would not be easy to find. Mr. Cox has a genius for expositions, which is very rare."—*Congregationalists.*

II.

BIBLICAL EXPOSITIONS.

Third Edition. Crown 8vo, cloth, price 8s. 6d.

"The tone of these homilies is wonderfully vigorous, and their standard surprisingly high. There are always the outlines of earnest thought to be traced under his most impassioned passages; and, so far as we have seen, he never quits a subject without illuminating it."—*Literary Churchman.*

III.

AN EXPOSITOR'S NOTE-BOOK.

Fourth Edition. Crown 8vo, cloth, price 8s. 6d.

"Mr. Cox's exegetical conscientiousness, fresh and unconventional thinking, tender sentiment, and fine literary taste, give a value to his papers which thoughtful minds and weary hearts will appreciate. We have only commendations for such a book."—*British Quarterly Review.*

Hodder and Stoughton,

D. L. MOODY AND HIS WORK.
BY REV. W. H. DANIELS, M.A., CHICAGO.
With Steel Engraving and Four Illustrations.
Third Edition, Crown 8vo, cloth, 3s. 6d.

"Mr. Daniels knew all about Mr. Moody's early life. The biographical part of his work is excellently done."—*Congregationalist.*

ROWLAND HILL:
HIS LIFE, ANECDOTES, AND PULPIT SAYINGS.
BY VERNON J. CHARLESWORTH.
With Introduction by C. H. SPURGEON. And Steel Portrait.
Sixth Thousand, fcap. 8vo, cloth, 3s. 6d.

"It is a rich and racy little volume, and will be eagerly read for its goodness, its wisdom and its wit."—*British Quarterly Review.*

ANECDOTES OF THE WESLEYS,
Illustrative of their Character and Personal History.
BY THE REV. J. B. WAKELEY, D.D.
Ninth Edition, fcap. 8vo, cloth, 3s. 6d.

"To all that are interested either in anecdote for its own sake or in anecdote illustrations of character it will be prized for the good things that it contains."—*British Quarterly Review.*

ANECDOTES OF REV. GEORGE WHITEFIELD, M.A.
With a Biographical Sketch. By the same Author.
Ninth Edition, fcap. 8vo, cloth, 3s. 6d.

"A goodly volume of 400 pages, in which the American author has gathered all that is known of this distinguished evangelist, and much that is new gathered from sources hitherto but little known."—*Weekly Review.*

ROBERT RAIKES,
JOURNALIST AND PHILANTHROPIST.
BY ALFRED GREGORY.
Fcap. 8vo, cloth, 3s. 6d.

"The life and character and career of this great and good man are traced in these pages with a firm and faithful hand, guided by an ardent sympathy with the great and good work he performed."—*Public Opinion.*

27, *Paternoster Row.*

THOMAS COOPER'S CHRISTIAN EVIDENCE SERIES.

I.

Nineteenth thousand, fcap. 8vo, 2s. 6d.

THE BRIDGE OF HISTORY OVER THE GULF OF TIME.

A Popular View of the Historical Evidence for the Truth of Christianity.

II.

Seventh Thousand, fcap. 8vo, cloth, 2s. 6d.

GOD, THE SOUL, AND A FUTURE STATE.

A twofold Popular Treatise. Containing (1) the combined Argument for the Being and Attributes of God ; and (2) the Argument for Man's Spiritual Nature and for a Future State.

III.

Fourth Thousand, fcap. 8vo, cloth, 2s. 6d.

THE VERITY OF CHRIST'S RESURRECTION FROM THE DEAD.

IV.

Fourth Thousand, fcap. 8vo, cloth, 2s. 6d.

THE VERITY AND VALUE OF THE MIRACLES OF CHRIST.

An Appeal to the Common Sense of the People.

V.

Second Thousand, fcap. 8vo, price 2s. 6d.

EVOLUTION, THE STONE BOOK,
AND THE
MOSAIC RECORD OF CREATION.

Hodder and Stoughton, 27, Paternoster Row.

Second Edition. Crown 8vo, cloth, price 7s. 6d.
FROM JERUSALEM TO ANTIOCH.
SKETCHES OF PRIMITIVE CHURCH LIFE.
BY THE REV. J. OSWALD DYKES, D.D.,
Author of "The Beatitudes of the Kingdom," etc.

"A treatise on the Acts of the Apostles from the ascension of the Lord to the foundation of the church in Antioch, preparatory to the mission work amongst the Gentiles—at once philosophical in its scope, critical in its method, popular in its style, and evangelical in its spirit."—*The late Rev. W. Arnot in "Family Treasury."*

"All who have heard Dr. Dykes will expect to find in these Expository Lectures on Acts i.—xii., much and clear thought, based on competent knowledge of his theme, expressed in a style of rare finish and beauty, and informed by a devout and refined spirit. Nor will they be disappointed. All these excellent qualities are happily displayed in the volume before us."—*Rev. Samuel Cox in "Expositor."*

Third Edition. Crown 8vo, price 5s.
ISRAEL'S IRON AGE:
SKETCHES FROM THE PERIOD OF THE JUDGES.
BY MARCUS DODS, D.D.,
Editor of Saint Augustine's Works, Author of "The Prayer that Teaches to Pray," etc.

"Powerful lectures. This is a noble volume, full of strength. Young men especially will find in it a rich storehouse of prevailing incentive to a godly life. Dr. Dods searches with a masterly hand."—*Nonconformist.*

Crown 8vo, cloth, price 7s. 6d.
THE HANDBOOK OF BIBLE GEOGRAPHY.
BY THE REV. GEORGE H. WITNEY, A.M.

Containing a Descriptive and Historical Account of every Place, Nation, and Tribe mentioned in the Bible and Apocrypha, Alphabetically arranged, and Illustrated by nearly One Hundred Engravings and Forty Maps and Plans.

"All that is known in regard to each place is mentioned briefly and succinctly, but accurately. The full-paged maps, of which there are twenty-two, are excellent. The engravings are exceedingly good."—*Christian Work.*

"Is worth procuring, if it was only for the maps: but it is really a repertory of most valuable information, evidently compiled with great care and conscientiousness, so as to be of the highest value."—*John Bull.*

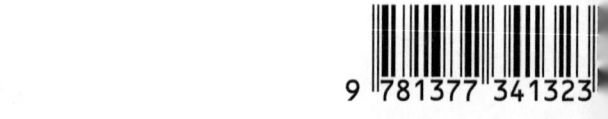

Lightning Source UK Ltd.
Milton Keynes UK
UKHW021909050619
343950UK00004B/64/P